Ben Holladay
The Stagecoach King

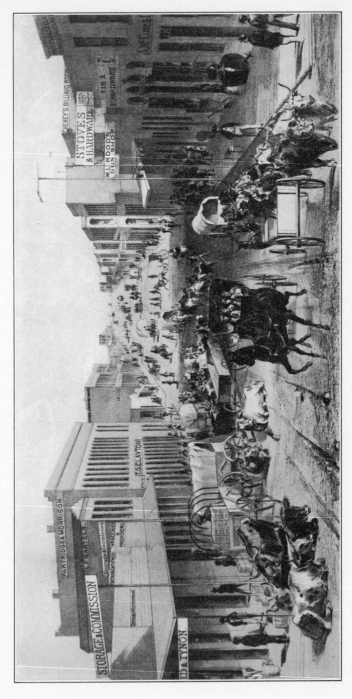

FIFTEENTH STREET, DENVER, 1865
From a contemporary drawing by A. E. Mathews

BEN HOLLADAY
THE STAGECOACH KING

A chapter in the development of
Transcontinental Transportation

by

J. V. FREDERICK, PH.D.
Northwestern State College, Alva, Oklahoma

THE ARTHUR H. CLARK COMPANY
Glendale, California, U.S.A.
1940

To
Doctor C. C. Rister

Contents

Preface

The Civil war produced in the west not battles and devastation, but primarily a grave necessity for maintaining and developing the vital lines of communication to the east. When early in the war the Overland Mail company was forced to abandon the southern route, the urgent need for communication was filled by Ben Holladay's efficient stagecoach service on the central route, which not only supplied the necessary link between east and west but led directly to the development of the newly settled regions beyond the Missouri river.

Between the years 1862 and 1866 Ben Holladay owned and operated a network of main and branch stagecoach lines from Kansas to California. Continuously faced by problems of bad weather, poor roads, highwaymen, and Indian raids, nevertheless the Holladay coaches maintained a regular schedule. Yet this vast enterprise and the man who guided it to success have been largely neglected except for scattered references in certain volumes relating to overland trade routes.

This volume was undertaken with the purpose of gathering and presenting new and unpublished information on the establishment and operation of Holladay's immense stagecoach system. Unfortunately, the original records of the Holladay Overland Mail and

Express company, lodged in the Wells, Fargo and company building in San Francisco, were destroyed by the earthquake and fire of 1906. The destruction of these records, coupled with the fact that the remaining contemporary material is so widely scattered, may account for the absence of any previous volume especially devoted to Holladay's stagecoach operations.

Careful research has been made through contemporary newspapers, original letters, family papers, and interviews with former employees and Holladay descendants. The author is indebted to many persons for their aid in the completion of this volume. Secretaries and librarians of the state historical societies in Oklahoma, Colorado, Nebraska, Kansas, and Montana have been very kind and helpful. Library staffs in the universities of Oklahoma, Kansas, and Nebraska and in the city libraries of Omaha and Kansas City, Missouri have permitted the author to study valuable materials. Officials in the Library of Congress and in many departments of the United States government have also aided in this research. To Miss Bennie Henry of Northwestern State college, Mrs. Elizbeth Copmann of Stillwater, and to his wife, who in many ways rendered valuable help during the preparation of this volume, the writer wishes to express his special gratitude.

Freighting in the West

Freighting in the West

On december 20, 1823 the *Missouri Intelligencer* advertised a three-day stagecoach service between St. Louis and Franklin. The speedy coach-and-four created a stir of excitement in eastern Missouri, accustomed to the slower parade of the wagon-trains, their bulging canvas-topped schooners drawn by three or four yoke of oxen, and with a train of bleating, braying, grunting, and bellowing livestock.[1] But the flurry caused by this new method of transportation soon subsided, for young Missouri was used to innovations and progress. Immigrants, by stagecoach, wagon-train, or afoot, were not a new sight along the Missouri river. Before the turn of the century Daniel Boone, the old crafty pioneer from Kentucky, had arrived in search of a new wilderness; during his manhood, in 1800, the land had passed from Spain to France, and, three years later, from France to the United States. It had become Missouri territory in 1812, and finally, in 1821, a new slave state. Already settlers from Virginia, Kentucky, Tennessee, and North Carolina had made their homes on the rich unbroken soil of Missouri. And others were joining their friends and kinsmen in a land where they believed their wealth in slaves to be secure.[2]

---

[1] *Missouri historical review,* XVII, 531; XXI, 36.

[2] Rader, *Civil government of U.S.,* 227; Riegel, *America moves west,* 26; Bogart, *Economic history of U.S.,* 73-77.

The explorer and adventurer of the old frontier were being replaced by the farmer and plantation owner. A man could live well and contentedly here in his rough log house and make one-third more profit than he had made in Kentucky. Land was cheap and abundantly productive. In the river-bottoms there was a rich black loam, sometimes thirty feet deep, and the supply of timber appeared to be limitless. The climate, too, was an attraction, for it went to no extremes and fostered no agues. Nor were the opportunities in Missouri limited to farming. The lucrative and thriving fur-trade, as well as that of the Mississippi river steamboat, had headquarters at St. Louis; the rich lead mines at the edge of the Ozark uplift employed hundreds of workers; boom town settlements, springing up along the Missouri river, were beginning to offer employment and a future to many newcomers.

With the growth of population and its spread toward the center of the state had come the need for mail service. By 1819 fifteen different mail routes had been established in Missouri territory, with weekly or bi-monthly deliveries, and post-offices were located at St. Louis, St. Charles, St. Genevieve, Cape Girardeau, and New Madrid.[3] Mail was carried more generally by steamboat on the Mississippi river than on the more treacherous Missouri, where floods were frequent and the river-bed shifted rapidly. Nevertheless, navigation of the Missouri on a commercial basis was necessary and inevitable. As the settlements

---

[3] Houck, *History of Missouri*, 63; *Missouri historical review*, XV, no. 1, 130.

since burned, cost him twelve thousand dollars) to the ladies of a Baptist church of which he was not a member, with the condition, however, that whenever the site was used for any but church purposes it should revert to his heirs.

It has been written that Holladay was an illiterate and coarse person, but the facts of his early life fail to substantiate this opinion. There is a legend that when he fell in love with a red-haired young beauty he was unable to gain her family's approval and forthwith eloped, taking the girl behind him on a speedy horse to the log cabin home of her uncle, where the marriage ceremony was performed. The story of family opposition and elopement has been denied, but it is a fact that in 1840, at the age of twenty-one, he was married to Ann Notley Calvert. Ann's family claimed descent from Lord Baltimore, founder of the Maryland colony. On the other hand, Holladay himself had local family distinction. His mother was a sister of General Andrew S. Hughes, instigator of the Platte purchase, which added six counties to the state of Missouri.[11]

Holladay was not destined merely to be the big man of a little town. In 1846 the Mexican war turned his interest toward transportation, and from that time on it became for him an absorbing career. Freighting seemed to promise more opportunities than stage-coaching, which was still greatly limited and in a somewhat primitive state. Drivers were paid only forty cents a day, and board; and the early stage roads were anything but highways. As there were no fences

[11] *Ibid.*

along the routes in Missouri the driver merely started
a new road over the prairie whenever he found the
old one too muddy. By 1839 there was a stage line
running eastward in Missouri from Independence,
and later a line ran across the state to Westport, the
future Kansas City. A rotund and jolly Colonel Lewis
operated this line, and its headquarters was the Westport Harris House.[12]

There was one stagecoach line, however, that ventured beyond the frontier. In july 1849 a line had been
started between Independence, Missouri, and Santa
Fe, New Mexico, then a newly acquired part of the
United States and a terminus of the important trade
route between that region and Missouri. The road led
through Indian lands by way of Council Grove.
Early coaches on the route were handsomely painted
and drawn by six mules. Eight guards, armed with
small Colt revolvers on belts, Colt revolving rifles,
long Colt revolvers, and hunting knives, protected the
passengers and guarded the United States mail. The
guards could fire one hundred thirty-six loads without
reloading.[13] Such precautions were very necessary
when a stagecoach ventured across the Indian's hunting ground.

It was over the old Santa Fe trail that General
Stephen W. Kearny and his army marched to the war
with Mexico in 1846. Supplies had to be shipped
from the Missouri river region to his troops in the
southwest. Here Holladay recognized his opportun-

---

[12] *Missouri historical review,* xv, no. 1, 130; Kansas City *times,* november 7, 1911.

[13] Inman, *Old Santa Fé trail,* 145-147.

ity; he secured a contract to supply Kearny with wagons, mules, bacon, and flour. Competition for such contracts was keen, but Holladay was successful. Prompt delivery and satisfactory merchandise made him a favorite contractor, and his profits were sometimes as high as two hundred per cent.[14]

At the close of the war in 1848, the United States acquired a vast expanse of western territory comprising the present California, Utah, Nevada, and portions of New Mexico, Arizona, Colorado, and Wyoming. Emigration to this region had long been checked by the menace of the Indian country beyond the Missouri frontier, but the indomitable pioneer impulse sent thousands of settlers to Oregon. The year before the end of the Mexican war saw another group of emigrants start for the west along the Oregon trail. The Mormons had again met opposition and mob violence, and their leader, Joseph Smith, had been killed. They had been forced to leave their Illinois home at Nauvoo, and now, under the guidance of Brigham Young, they sought a new promised land. Late in july 1847, on the isolated shores of the Great Salt lake of Utah, they founded their settlement.

The following year gold was discovered in California, and among the thousands of excited fortune-seekers coming west by wagon-train, many of the braver ones took a short cut through Salt Lake City. Soon they were making stop-overs in order to replenish supplies, sometimes dangerously depleted by the unexpected hardships of the journey. Most of the

14 *Catholic tribune* (St. Joseph, Mo.), june 22, 1895.

supplies for the emigrants, as well as those used in the
Mormon community itself, had to be shipped overland from Missouri, and here Holladay saw a new
opportunity. At the close of the war the government
was left with surplus supplies on its hands and had
sold them at a very low price. Holladay, with the
profits of his government contracts, bought oxen and
wagons. By february 1849 he was able to start on a
venture in freighting. His plan was to take a wagon-
train of goods over the twelve hundred miles to the
Mormon settlement, and for this purpose he formed
a partnership with Theodore W. Warner, one of
Weston's leading merchants. Warner was to furnish
the trade goods and Holladay the oxen and wagons.[15]

Fifty wagons, filled with seventy thousand dollars
worth of merchandise, made this first venturesome
trip. Holladay was gambling with his Mexican war
fortune; one disastrous Indian attack, bad storms
along the trail, or an unfavorable reception by the
Mormons would have meant failure. The huge wide-
wheeled freight wagons with their accompaniment of
auxiliary livestock and men followed the Oregon
trail through South pass. The trail led through the
tall prairie grass of Kansas and eastern Nebraska territory, where there was an abundance of food, fuel,
and water. Then beyond the paradise of the South
Platte the scene changed. The air grew lighter, the
road through the sagebrush and cactus gradually
tilted upward. Alkali dust burned throats and poi-
soned drinking-water. But this was good buffalo
country, where all travelers looked forward to meet-

---

15 *Ibid.;* Paxton, *Annals of Platte county,* 110, 119.

ing a herd with the hope of feasting on fresh meat and
replenishing their supplies. Indian attacks were less
pleasantly anticipated. At night, with the wagons
gathered together to form a protective corral for the
stock, the men took turns keeping watch. All firearms
were loaded. Although Indian attacks were not so frequent as they were to become, the tales of horror
drifting back from one such affair were enough to
keep every traveler on the alert. Even though the Indian did no more than start a stampede of cattle, he
was a troublesome enemy. At Fort Laramie there was
the relief of meadows and good camping. Then the
desert and more alkali. Beyond Jim Bridger's trading-post the trail followed the Sweetwater river, ran
for a few miles through the "bad lands," and went on
through the easy mountain grades of South pass. A
little beyond, Holladay's wagon-train left the Oregon
trail and turned southwest, going down through the
mountain canyons and on to Salt Lake City in the
valley of the Great Salt lake.

Holladay reached his destination without great
mishap. He was armed with a letter to Brigham
Young from his former colonel, now General Alexander Doniphan, hero of the Mexican war, who had led
the expedition against the Mormons at Far West
eleven years before. The letter reminded the Mormon
leader that Holladay had been friendly to his people
at that time, and asked fair treatment for him. Young
received Holladay and blessed him. In a sermon before his people the following sunday, he said,
"Brother Holladay has a large stock of goods for sale
and can be trusted as an honorable dealer." These

were golden words, and when after the services Brigham Young broke bread with Holladay and his men, the seventy thousand dollars worth of merchandise was as good as sold. Within a few days the entire stock had been disposed of at a large profit.[16]

There was many a heated argument in those days over the respective merits of certain trails, and often wagon-trains were split because of disagreement. Holladay was not satisfied with the road between Fort Bridger and Salt Lake City, and decided before his return to discover a new one. This was one of the few Holladay ventures to prove unsuccessful. With a negro man and two mules he set out hopefully enough but lost his bearings, and they wandered about the mountains until the food supply was exhausted. After several days they found a broken-down buffalo, the flesh of which sustained them until familiar landmarks were reached. Holladay said later that this particular buffalo was the sweetest food he had ever tasted.[17]

Upon his return to Weston in the fall of 1849, Holladay used some of the profits of his Salt Lake venture to buy, in company with three other men, a large tract of land near the town. He also purchased the Union mills on the Platte river, possibly encouraged in this enterprise by the success of his brother David, who owned a mill and distillery near Weston. Ben was now a man of position and importance, and quite naturally chose this time to build an imposing home, one that would especially please his beloved

16 *Catholic tribune* (St. Joseph, Mo.), june 22, 1895.
17 *Ibid.*

wife. So on a high sloping hill east of Weston there arose a pretentious brick mansion with stone window cornices. It had sixteen large rooms, a spacious yard, and an even more spacious stable. In addition, Holladay owned a twelve hundred acre farm near Union Mills, now Edgerton, Missouri. Home, farm, stores, and factories would have been sufficient to absorb the time and energies of an average man, but not the ambitious Holladay.[18]

The freighting business, with its uncertainties, its dangers, and its profits, appealed strongly to him. In 1850 he and Warner sent out a wagon-train to Utah territory carrying goods to the value of one hundred and fifty thousand dollars. The second venture was as successful as the first. On this trip the two freighters opened a small store in an adobe schoolhouse in Salt Lake City. Later the stock was moved to a larger building opposite the south gate of Temple block, under the management of William H. Hooper, whose wife was a Mormon. Prices were high at that time. Some examples were:

Brown shirting and sheeting	20c to 30c a yard
Kentucky jeans	25c to $1.25
Cotton flannel	30c to 40c a yard
Prints	25c to 50c a yard
Wheat	75c to $1.00 a bushel
Glass	$15 to $18 a half box
Foolscap and letter paper	$10 to $12 a ream [19]

On this second trip Holladay gambled, with for-

[18] Holladay, Hattie, interview with author, 1, 2, MS.

[19] Bancroft, *History of Utah*, 762; Tullidge, *History of Salt Lake City*, I, 354, 370.

tuitous results, on a trip west from Salt Lake City. He traded goods for a herd of cattle and drove them from Utah to California. The trip from Salt Lake City promised more peril than any he had yet experienced, and many before him had perished while making their way through the mountains. He got through with little loss, however, and drove his herd down into the valley of the Sacramento. There he fattened his cattle on the rich grass and bided his time. He soon discovered that they were short of cattle in that part of the country and the market was bare. But he did not hasten to take advantage of his good fortune in the usual way. Instead he sold a few cattle to the rich Panama Steamship company at a comparatively low price and waited for the buyers to make the next move. He knew that they had to have more beef. Soon the superintendent of the company summoned him. Holladay sent back word that he had no time to come to them and that they must come to him. They came, and paid thirty cents a pound on the hoof for the rest of his cattle, which he had bought at six dollars a head. This bit of clever dickering afforded him as much pleasure as it did money; and he afterward admitted that he had wanted very badly to go to the company and sell them his cattle, that he would even have crawled there, but that he had very firmly resisted the temptation.[20]

Holladay continued in the cattle business but did not give up freighting. In 1853 he contracted to supply the Benicia barracks post in California with fresh beef for a year. In writing to the commissary-general

[20] *Catholic tribune* (St. Joseph, Mo.), june 22, 1895.

The Central Overland Route

Before the United States government established an overland mail route, the operation of stagecoach lines west of the Mississippi was limited in extent. In 1847 express lines had been running in California on a weekly service between San Francisco and Sutter's fort but had met little success. After the discovery of gold in 1848 an overland mule-train express, called the "California Star Express," was operated for a short time. The line was promoted by Samuel Braman, publisher of the *California Star*. He planned to give a sixty-day service between Independence, Missouri, and San Francisco by way of Salt Lake City. St. Louis men also attempted to establish an overland mail and passenger line about 1849, but the project was abandoned after one difficult trip.[37]

To the settler in isolated communities, far from news of the outside world, the most vital problem of the day was mail delivery, and he kept the government reminded of its responsibility in this respect through letters, newspaper editorials, and impassioned speeches. The government saw the necessity for this bond between east and west, but conditions of roads and weather on the land route made even a monthly mail delivery uncertain.

However, in 1848 the United States government

[37] Winther, *Express and stage-coach days in California*, 18, 19.

began service on the central route. Arrangements were made for a monthly service over the twelve hundred miles between Independence and Salt Lake City. The stagecoach was not in general use as a carrier until ten years later and this first mail delivery was made by one set of pack mules. No change of animals was made during the thirty days of travel. The postal department awarded this first contract to Samuel H. Woodson of Independence, Missouri, for nineteen thousand five hundred dollars a year.[38]

In 1851 Woodson contracted with Feramorz Little of Salt Lake City to carry the mail between that settlement and Fort Laramie. As only the trading-post of Jim Bridger, one hundred miles away, lay between these widely separated points, it was a difficult assignment. Little has recorded, with reminiscent amusement, his first trip west from Fort Laramie in company with his Indian partner, Ephraim Hanks. His pack animals, having made the trip from Salt Lake City to Fort Laramie in nine days, were too weary for the return trip. Consequently, Little, unable to substitute domestic animals, was obliged to take five wild Mexican mules from a near-by rancher. The mules had to be thrown, tied, and blinded before they could be harnessed. After the four had been hitched to the wagon and the fifth saddled, Little got into the wagon and Hanks mounted the saddle mule. The blinders were removed and the fun began. For eight miles over the Black hills the mules tried to escape from their burdens, braying, bucking, kicking over the traces, and generally exhibiting the tenden-

---

[38] Burton, *City of the saints*, 4; *Philatelic gossip*, VIII, 353.

cies of their kind. Hanks and Little had nothing to do but hold on until the animals tired.

Operating under such difficulties, they were often unable to deliver the mail according to schedule. On one trip these two lost their best mules and ran out of food. For five days they lived upon parched corn. At another time, in the winter of 1852, they were lost near South pass for several days, and for over a month were struggling through the snows. Forced to abandon their horses, they cachéd the heavy mail and dragged the letter mail through the drifts of the Wasatch mountains, walking forty miles in all.[39]

It is difficult to understand, in view of these facts, why the next contract for monthly mail service should have been for an even lower amount, fourteen thousand four hundred dollars, unless it was a deliberately low bid to insure getting the contract. This was issued in 1854 to M. F. McGraw. That year McGraw, in addition to the usual weather difficulties, encountered loss and destruction from Indian attacks. He asked the government for relief, and the following year's contract was raised to thirty-six thousand dollars. As indemnity for the property losses, Congress in may 1856 appropriated seventeen thousand seven hundred and fifty dollars. The contract was renewed for a third year, but the people of Utah were complaining that the service was unsatisfactory and demanding a change. Consequently it was declared that the contract would be annulled upon its expiration august 18, 1856.[40]

[39] *Ibid.;* Burton, *op. cit.,* 4.
[40] *Ibid.; Philatelic gossip,* VIII, 353; U.S. *Statutes at large,* x, 684.

The Mormons were anxious to take over the problem of a proper mail and express route. Some time before this, at a meeting in the Salt Lake tabernacle, a movement had been started under the direction of their leader, Brigham Young, to establish a great express line from the Missouri river to the Pacific coast. Apparently they recognized the value of the stagecoach in mail delivery. There had been constant opposition to its use, for it was believed that the single horse or mule was swifter and that mails would be delayed for repair of coaches. Young planned to equip the entire route with stagecoach stops at intervals along the line. His dream was to be realized before another decade had passed, but as a Mormon enterprise it was never accomplished.

Nevertheless the B.Y. Express company was organized, and in 1856 a Mormon agent for that company, Hiram Kimball, was awarded a contract for twenty-three thousand dollars for monthly service between the Missouri river and Salt Lake City. This contractor specified in his bid that he would use mules or horses, wagons or carriages for his transportation. However, Kimball was unable to perform the service of the 1856 contract, as the United States government claimed that he had not been ready in time to fulfill the obligation as promised. Feramorz Little and Ephraim Hanks, awarded a special contract in the emergency, made only one trip east. They left Salt Lake City december 11, 1856, and reached Independence february 27. In the meantime the B.Y. Express company had been working on the trail, building stations and settlements; in march one of its carriers,

John R. Murdock, went from Salt Lake City to Independence in fifteen days, making only three changes of animals. He commenced his return trip about may 1, with several wagon-loads of mail for the west.[41]

At this time the Mormon war intervened and terminated the plans of the B.Y. Express company. M. F. McGraw, Kimball's unsuccessful predecessor in the mail service, was an aggressor in the movement against the Mormons and one of the signers of the letter to President Buchanan, which described unfavorably the state of affairs in Utah territory. Communication with Salt Lake City was cut off and weekly service between Fort Bridger and Independence commenced. This contract paid a compensation of $15,833 a month.[42] As soon as the Utah matter was adjusted, a contract for monthly service from Salt Lake City was awarded to S. B. Miles, at $32,000 a year. The contract stipulated that Miles use four-horse coaches between the months of april and december, although during the rest of the year he was allowed to carry the mail on the more convenient pack-mule.[43]

Between 1851 and 1858 various attempts had been made to carry the mail overland from Salt Lake City to California. The steamer route to California and Oregon from the east was greatly preferred, since it

[41] Burton, *City of the saints,* 4; U.S. House. *Executive documents,* 35 cong., 1 sess., XI, no. 96, 353.

[42] U.S. *Statutes at large,* XI, 248; *Philatelic gossip,* VIII, 353; U.S. House. *Executive documents,* 35 cong., 1 sess., XI, no. 96, 353; 2 sess., XI, no. 109, 856. McGraw is also sometimes spelled Magraw.

[43] U. S. *Statutes at large,* XI, 248; *Philatelic gossip,* VIII, 353; U.S. House. *Executive documents,* 35 cong., 1 sess., XI, no. 96, 353; 2 sess., XI, no. 109, 856.

was more certain than the hazardous route through the mountains. With the increasing need of a more direct communication between the gold fields and Salt Lake City came service on the central route. The trail led from Sacramento to Placerville, thence to Carson valley and the Humboldt, through the Goose Creek mountains and southeast to Salt Lake City. The bare recorded facts of these trips are eloquent. On the first trip from Sacramento, may 1, 1851, the contractors, Absalom Woodward and George Chorpenning, reached Salt Lake City june 5, after having beaten a trail with wooden mauls through the deep snows of the Sierras. On his way with the november mails Woodward was killed by Indians. In december and january carriers had to turn back, defeated by the elements. In february their horses were frozen to death in the Goose Creek mountains, and they walked the last two hundred miles to Salt Lake City, having made the entire trip in sixty days.[44]

In 1853 it was decided to give up these attempts and to change the mail route so that it would run south to Los Angeles and northeast to Salt Lake City. This change cut off the busy Carson valley section, and monthly mail service had to be arranged between the valley and Placerville. The carriers were forced to travel on snowshoes. Legends have grown up in that vicinity concerning one "Snowshoe Thompson," a Norwegian, who wore snowshoes ten feet long and in two days carried one hundred pounds of mail from Placerville to Carson.[45]

By 1858 extensive increases in western mail lines

[44] Bancroft, *History of Nevada, Colorado, and Wyoming*, 226.
[45] Hafen, *Overland mail*, 65; Bancroft, *op. cit.*, 226, 227.

were being made, and service on the central route
west from Salt Lake City was resumed. George Chorpenning, who had done much to interest the government in improving the service, was given the new
contract. It was for one hundred and thirty thousand
dollars a year on a sixteen-day schedule. The route
between Missouri and Utah territory was given to
John M. Hockaday for one hundred and ninety thousand dollars a year for a weekly service of four-mule
carriages or wagons on a twenty-two day schedule.
When through mail service was established in july of
that year, the mails were carried from Missouri to
California in thirty-two to thirty-four days.[46]

Dissatisfaction with conditions along the central
route continued. The subject of a selected, govern-
ment-subsidized mail route was under debate, and
every western congressman was interested in securing
the line for his own district. Some opponents said that
natural conditions on the central route were against
any permanent and satisfactory service. Californians,
on the other hand, were dissatisfied with the ocean
mail service. The Pacific Mail Steamship company
with its $724,350 contract held a monopoly, and it was
thought that strong competition would result in low-
ered prices and better service, both to passengers and
to the large crowds of pioneers and miners who
waited at the dock for mail on the bi-monthly
"steamer day." [47]

[46] U.S. House. *Executive documents,* 33 cong., 2 sess., no. 86, 711; 35
cong., 2 sess., XI, no. 109, 501, 863; U.S. *Statutes at large,* XI, 521; Postmaster-general's *report,* 1858, in U.S. Senate. *Executive documents,* 35
cong., 2 sess., IV, no. 1, part 4, 722.
[47] U.S. *Congressional globe,* 34 cong., 3 sess., appendix, 315; U.S.
Statutes at large, XI, 248. The cost of the mail service in 1857 between

Congress at this time authorized Postmaster-general Aaron V. Brown to entertain bids for a letter service from the Mississippi river to San Francisco, the contract to be for a period of six years at not over three hundred thousand dollars a year for weekly, or six hundred thousand dollars for semi-weekly service. Among the bids were proposals for several different routes. Some were for the Salt Lake City line, some for a northern trail from St. Paul to San Francisco, and others for a southern route. When the contract was awarded to an eastern company, represented by John Butterfield of Utica, New York, and William G. Fargo of Buffalo, it was announced that the route would go from St. Louis and Memphis to El Paso and San Francisco.[48]

There was an immediate cry of "partisanship!" The southern route was forty per cent longer than the others and had not been the selection of any of the bidders. The fact that Postmaster-general Brown was from Tennessee and strongly sympathetic to the south seemed to confirm the suspicion. Given the power to select his contractors, in this case he had also selected his route. Every one of the contractors, however, had agreed to follow the route if his bid should be accepted. In defense of his choice Brown reminded his critics of the failures on the Salt Lake City route and of the impracticability, on the same grounds, of the

New York and San Francisco was: New York to Charleston, Savannah, New Orleans, Havana, Chagres, and back—$261,000; transportation across the isthmus of Panama—$135,000; Panama to California, Oregon, and back—$328,350.

48 *American almanac,* 1858, chap. 96, 142; Postmaster-general's *report,* 1857, in U.S. Senate. *Executive documents,* 35 cong., 1 sess., IV, no. 11, 988, 989, 994-997.

suggested one through Albuquerque. He praised the comfort and safety of what one New York paper called the "ox-bow" route, mentioning its ideal weather conditions and its convenient location with respect to Mexico.[49]

The press of east, north, and west protested in vain. The "outrage," the "foul wrong," "one of the greatest swindles ever perpetrated upon the country by slave-holders" was finally accepted as inevitable. Work toward improvement of the route continued. Finally, on september 15, 1858, the first stagecoaches left San Francisco and St. Louis. When they arrived at their respective destinations ahead of time they were met by brass bands, loud hurrahs, and louder speeches. The western trip required twenty-four days, eighteen hours, and twenty-five minutes, and the east-bound coach arrived at St. Louis after twenty-three days and four hours.[50]

President Buchanan sent the following telegram to Butterfield, for whom the new route was named:

I cordially congratulate you upon the result. It is a glorious triumph for civilization and the union. Settlements will soon follow the course of the road, and the East and the West will be bound together by a chain of living Americans which can never be broken.[51]

Within three years "the glorious triumph for civilization" was to be abandoned because of war within

[49] Ibid., 994-997, 1000, 1005, 1011; Sacramento daily union, october 16, 1858. This issue contains the papers of F. W. Lander relating to early roads and mail lines in the west.

[50] Missouri republican (St. Louis), october 11, 1858; Weekly Missouri democrat (St. Louis), october 15, 1858; Postmaster-general's report, 1858, 739, 740.

[51] Root and Connelley, Overland stage, 13.

the union, but the "chain of living Americans" was to remain unbroken throughout the war, partly through the efforts of Holladay in maintaining his stage line on the central route during the trouble.

Although Postmaster-general Brown had shown evidence of partiality toward the south, he had in general considered the postal department a pioneer of civilization rather than a self-supporting business. His generous attitude was appreciated when after his death his successor, Postmaster-general Joseph Holt, reduced the Hockaday-Liggett weekly service to semi-monthly.

During the excitement over the Butterfield route the Pike's Peak region had been booming. Gold had been discovered, and the excited fortune-seekers were pouring in. Denver, the largest settlement in the region, was two hundred miles from the nearest post-office at Fort Laramie. An occasional express brought long-delayed letters, at fifty cents each, to the miners in the vicinity. It was at this point that William H. Russell, of the freighting firm of Russell, Majors, and Waddell, believed that he saw an excellent opportunity to establish a stagecoach express between Leavenworth and Denver. Russell was the impetuous member of the firm, and Majors the conservative. Finding Majors unwilling to join him in the enterprise, Russell went into partnership with John S. Jones of Missouri. With ninety-day personal notes Russell and Jones bought one thousand Kentucky mules and fifteen Concord coaches. The firm took the name, the Leavenworth and Pike's Peak Express company. Service started on may 17, 1859, over the six hundred eighty-seven mile route. The course was from Leavenworth to Fort Riley, to the Smoky Hill fork of the Kansas river, northward and westward to a point twenty miles from the mouth of Cherry creek, and then to Denver. Stations were built every ten or fifteen miles. Soon daily coaches were running in each direction, making the trip in six days at an average speed of one hundred miles in twenty-four hours.[52]

When the Leavenworth and Pike's Peak Express had been operating less than a month, the firm of Jones and Russell enlarged its route by purchasing the mail contract of Hockaday and Liggett for fifty thousand dollars. The latter company was losing about sixty thousand dollars a year because of Postmaster-general Holt's reduction in their service. Its equipment was appraised and bought for ninety-four thousand dollars. Jones and Russell now had a mail route from Missouri to Salt Lake City and their contract paid one hundred thirty thousand dollars a year. Prospects were excellent and might have remained so had the rush to the Pike's Peak region continued. What the conservative Majors probably had foreseen now happened. During the summer of 1859 the rush began to subside. Expenses of operation overbalanced receipts, and Jones and Russell were unable to pay their ninety-day notes. To protect Russell the freighting firm of Russell, Majors, and Waddell was forced to take over their holdings.[53]

The freighting route of the firm had gone through

---

[52] Majors, *Seventy years on the frontier*, 164; Parsons, *Making of Colorado*, 142.

[53] Majors, *op. cit.*, 165; *Weekly Leavenworth* (Kans.) *herald*, may 28, september 3, 1859; Atchison (Kans.) *union*, june 18, 1859.

Atchison and along the Platte river valley. The Jones and Russell stagecoach route, on the other hand, had been along the Smoky Hill fork of the Kansas river. There was a spirited rivalry between the young towns of Atchison and Leavenworth in Kansas territory, and Leavenworth logically hoped that under the new regime the Smoky Hill route, which started from Leavenworth, would be retained. Majors had always preferred the Platte river route for freighting. He maintained that the river sand purified the water which the low banks made easily accessible. Grass was so plentiful along the way to the South Platte that no other food was necessary for the animals, while oxen and buffalo chips provided an abundance of fuel. In defense of the South Platte road Majors said:

There is no other route in the United States, nor in my opinion, elsewhere, of the same length, where such numbers of men and animals could travel during the summer season as could over the thoroughfare from the Missouri river up the Platte and its tributaries to the Rocky mountains.[54]

Leavenworth citizens pointed out that the road from their city to Pike's Peak was less than four hundred miles long, while the road by way of Atchison and Fort Kearny to Pike's Peak was six hundred fifty-five miles, as measured by Colonel Jones in 1859. They also argued that the grass appeared earlier and lasted longer on the Smoky Hill route. Citizens along the trail were asked to subscribe money, oxen, and other property to a fund which was to help advertise their route. So enterprising were these pioneer city boosters that twenty-one hundred sixty-five dollars

54 Majors, op. cit., 145-148.

was collected from Auburn, Topeka, Lawrence, Junction City, Manhattan, and Fort Riley. To provide money to help in this advertising campaign the Leavenworth city council issued three thousand dollars in bonds and offered them for sale. However, the campaign left the firm of Russell, Majors, and Waddell unconvinced, and soon after it became the owner of the Leavenworth and Pike's Peak Express, the Smoky Hill route was abandoned for the favored Platte river trail.[55]

Improved service followed the change of ownership. Stages that had made the trip in twenty-one days now reached their destination in ten. Daily service was established. One hundred new stations were built. Hay and grain and newly purchased livestock were kept in new stables. Besides the one thousand Kentucky mules now used for regular stage work there were three hundred smaller mules to haul the lighter coaches in the mountain regions.[56] In 1860 the Kansas territorial legislature granted a charter to Russell, Majors, and Waddell. The firm was to be called by the new title of Central Overland California and Pike's Peak Express company. The term was immediately curtailed to the C.O.C. & P.P. EXP. CO. The principal office was to be in Leavenworth, unless a vote of two-thirds of the directors should change the location. Members of the corporation were William H. Russell, John S. Jones, Ben F. Ficklin, Alexander Majors, Benjamin C. Card, William B. Wad-

[55] *Ibid.*, 165; Leavenworth (Kans.) *daily conservative*, june 2, 1860.

[56] Majors, *Seventy years on the frontier*, 148, 166. See also Elwell, "Story of the overland mail" in *Frontier days*, 423-425.

dell, John W. Russell, Luther R. Smoot, and their associates, assigns, and successors. Permission was given by the charter to issue a capital stock of five hundred thousand dollars to be divided into shares of one hundred dollars each. The charter permitted the company to

establish, maintain, and operate any express, stage, passenger, or transportation route or routes, by land or water, for the conveyance of persons, mails, and property from, to, and between any place in Kansas, and any place in or beyond the limits of Kansas. . .

It was a liberal charter. The firm was empowered to build and keep warehouses and storehouses, to insure property against fire and other hazards of transportation. It could also explore lands for minerals and mine and refine gold and other metals. It was allowed to draw, make, accept, endorse, or guarantee drafts or bills of exchange, and to buy, sell, and negotiate the same. In addition, the firm could receive gold and other money, or other valuables on deposit at any of its places of business, and make money orders for payment or delivery of same at any other places at which it did business.[57]

Russell, Majors, and Waddell, aided by this liberal charter, had reason to expect success in their venture. They had not, however, taken sufficiently into account the promoting enthusiasm of William Russell. Early in 1860 Russell, in Washington on a business trip, was persuaded by Senator William Gwin of California to start a pony express on the central route. The idea behind this venture was to induce congress

---

[57] Kansas territorial *laws*, 1860, chap. 143, 254.

to grant the firm a mail contract on that line by proving its feasibility for transportation. The Butterfield route was at this time the government's choice, but the advocates of a central route could not accept the decision as final. Majors, characteristically, did not entirely favor the idea, but he gave his support to Russell.

On april 3, 1860, a great crowd gathered near the Pike's Peak stable at St. Joseph, Missouri, to see the start of the pony express. It was a super fourth-of-july occasion, with flags and bands, speeches and excitement. At the boom of a cannon the rider (whether Billy Richardson or Johnny Fry historians cannot be sure) rode to the post-office. A square leather packet with four padlocked pockets was given to him. He crossed the Missouri river on a ferry and sped westward to meet the next carrier forty miles away. Each succeeding carrier maintained a rapid pace during the next ten and one-half days. The last rider was treated to an exhibition of gratitude, band-playing, and flag-waving enthusiasm which lasted until after midnight.[58]

The management of the pony express was in Russell's hands, while B. F. Ficklin supervised the business at Salt Lake City, and W. W. Finney at San Francisco. Although it paved the way for future mail contracts over the central route, and provided material for pageant and motion picture in the years to come, the pony express was not a successful venture

[58] *Rocky mountain news* (Denver), february 15, 1860; Bradley, *Pony express*, 14, 15, 20, 23, 30, 31, 39; Majors, *Seventy years on the frontier*, 174, 182, 183; Visscher, *Pony express*, 32.

financially, as the following figures clearly indicate:

To equip line	$100,000
Maintenance for 16 months	480,000
Indian war	75,000
Other expenses	45,000
	$700,000

Receipts during the period of operation had been two hundred thousand dollars.

In Nevada territory the Washoe Indians had opposed the pony express as an agent for the white settlers. During may 1860 they made attacks, burning stations and stealing livestock. Their protest against the white man's invasion was so vigorous that Russell, Majors, and Waddell were obliged to defend their property by armed force. Volunteers enlisted to fight in the war, and all expenses were paid by the company. By june 25 the regular schedule had been resumed, but a new enemy was yet to enter the field. Swift as the pony express had been, it could not compete with the telegraph. On october 24, 1861, the telegraph line from Nebraska territory to the Pacific coast was completed. There was no further use for the gallant relay of pony riders.[59]

The pony express had served its purpose, that of proving to the government the worth of the central route. The Butterfield company, however, not Russell, Majors, and Waddell, gathered the first fruits

[59] Root and Connelley, *Overland stage,* 122; San Francisco *daily evening bulletin,* may 26, 28, june 2, 9, 25, 1860; Atchison (Kans.) *union,* october 26, 1861; Postmaster-general's *report,* 1861, in U.S. Senate. *Executive documents,* 37 cong., 2 sess., III, part 3, no. 1, 560.

of the effort. A serious turn of affairs had brought the central route back into favor; seven southern states had withdrawn from the union between december 1860 and february 1861. Part of the Civil war was being fought in the vicinity of the Butterfield route, and the stage line was forced to discontinue service through Texas.

On march 2, 1861, congress passed an act authorizing the postmaster-general to stop the postal service on any route or part of any route whenever he found the service threatened. Section 9 of this act authorized discontinuance of route no. 12578, the Butterfield line, by july 1, 1861. The Butterfield company was not thrown out of business by the act, but was required to move northward to the central route for transportation of the entire letter mail. A part of the mail was to be carried between a point on the Missouri river and Placerville on a twenty-three day schedule during the eight months of the year, mails to be delivered tri-weekly to Denver and Salt Lake City. The rest was to be carried between Missouri and California in thirty-five days, thus allowing the firm to carry that mail semi-monthly by ocean route from New York to San Francisco, provided that the trip by steamer could be made in twenty-five days. The company was also to run the pony express until the telegraph line should be completed. These trips were to be made on a ten-day schedule during eight months of the year and on a twelve-day schedule during the other four months.[60]

---

[60] *Ibid.*, 560, 561; U.S. *Statutes at large*, XII, 206; U.S. *Congressional globe*, 36 cong., 2 sess., part I, 1112.

The modified contract paid one million dollars a year to the mail carrier from march 25, 1861, to july 1, 1864. A further agreement was made that the company was to receive regular pay during the time when its livestock and other equipment were being moved to the central route, as well as extra pay on their old contract because of the property lost by the change. This pay was set at the amount the firm had received for two months of service under the old contract. Russell, Majors, and Waddell were not overlooked in the agreement. It was arranged that the Central Overland California and Pike's Peak Express company should handle the mail and run the pony express between Atchison and Salt Lake City, while the Butterfield company handled the transportation between Salt Lake City and Placerville.[61]

Postmaster-general Holt, primarily a business man, was a bitter foe of the central route. In 1861 the United States government had spent $1,228,241 for the maintenance of mail lines between the east and California and had received only $296,496.71 from the business. The central route had cost $208,241 and returned only $5,284.14. Holt now said that it would require an appropriation of $600,000 a year to maintain a daily mail service. In fact, he did not want such a service, as he felt that it would benefit only the contractors. He predicted failure for the plan.[62]

61 *Ibid.;* Postmaster-general's *report,* 1861, 560, 561.

62 *Ibid.,* 1860, in U.S. Senate. *Executive documents,* 36 cong., 2 sess., III, part 3, no. 1, 436. The expenses and receipts of Pacific routes in 1860 were:

ROUTE	EXPENSES	RECEIPTS
New York to San Francisco by ocean	$350,000.00	$170,825.40

Within three months service was begun on the new route. On the first day of july 1861 a stagecoach left St. Joseph. It reached San Francisco on the evening of july 18. This was at least three days shorter than the southern route time. Stagecoaches now began to be accompanied by soldiers. The Civil war had drawn upon the regular troops and as Indian uprisings were feared the war department sent one regiment and five additional companies of soldiers from California to take their place.[63]

Russell, Majors, and Waddell were jubilant over their future prospects. They had been in a precarious financial situation for some time. The C.O.C. & P.P. firm had become known to its employees as the "Clean Out of Cash and Poor Pay." It was over four hundred thousand dollars in debt. There were few stations on the line, and the equipment was poor. General Bela M. Hughes had accepted the presidency of the company on april 26, 1861, unaware of the company's financial difficulties.[64] Certain records show that in may and june of that year Russell, Majors, and Waddell had begun to borrow money from Holladay to secure better equipment for its line, though it is possible that the firm had started its loans from Holladay two years earlier. When more money was needed by the company to meet current expenditures, Holladay

ROUTE	EXPENSES	RECEIPTS
Overland by way of El Paso	600,000.00	119,766.76
St. Joseph to Salt Lake City	125,000.00	4,305.64
Salt Lake City to Placerville	83,241.00	978.50
San Antonio to Stockton	70,000.00	593.41

[63] San Francisco *daily evening bulletin*, august 3, 1861; Postmaster-general's *report*, 1861, 560.

[64] *Freedom's champion* (Atchison, Kans.), december 23, 1861.

refused to advance it without mortgage for security, so on july 5 the directors ordered a mortgage placed upon the entire line and its equipment. Holladay then made further loans, for the stagecoach line was not paying running expenses. On november 21 the firm executed a deed of trust for the payment of four hundred thousand dollars, and in december an advertisement in a Leavenworth paper read as follows:

T. F. Warner and Robert L. Pease advertise to sell, under a deed of trust on the thirty-first day of this month, all the horses, mules, cattle, coaches, and other property belonging to the Central Overland California and Pike's Peak company.

Creditors attempted to secure an injunction, whereupon the judge of the Kansas circuit court ordered a delay in the date of sale. The company now expected no interference before the first of april, and the contractors went ahead with their business. Conditions at the time looked promising for a recovery, but a severe winter and the decrease of passengers brought further discouragement. Late in december fares were much reduced. Each passenger was allowed twenty-five pounds of baggage free, and stop-overs without extra charge. Coaches were running as usual in january 1862. However, in february the stage line was again advertised for sale at Atchison, and the auction was held on march 21.

It was Holladay who made the highest bid, one hundred thousand dollars, for the property. Later, explaining his part in the sale, he said that he had been obliged to protect his investment. Russell, Majors, and Waddell at this time owed him two hundred and eight thousand dollars. In a letter from Washing-

Line." The following two stanzas are but samples of
the innumerable verses of this song.

DRIVER'S SONG

Verse 5

> You ask me for our leader, I'll soon inform you, then;
> It's Holladay they call him, and often only Ben;
> If you can read the papers, it's easy work to scan.
> He beats the world in staging now, or any other man!

Chorus

> Statesmen and warriors, traders and the rest
> May boast of their profession and think it is the best.
> Their taste I'll never envy, I'll have you understand
> Long as I can be a driver on the jolly overland.

Verse 11

> It's thus you're safely carried throughout the mighty West,
> Where chances to make fortunes are ever famed the best.
> And thus the precious pouches of mail are brought to hand
> Through the ready hearts that center in the jolly overland.

The drivers' loyalty to Holladay was second to no
other. It is said that Governor Alexander Cummings
of Colorado territory once tried to bribe one of them
to drive faster. The man told him emphatically that
he had been hired by Holladay to drive that coach,
and he was driving to please Holladay, with proper
respect to the interests of the company.

The most far-famed of all the Holladay drivers
was Buffalo Bill Cody. For a time, he drove between
Plum Creek, Nebraska territory, and Fort Kearny.
He also drove in Dakota territory on the line between
Three Crossings and Split Rock. On one trip in the
latter region his coach was suddenly attacked by sev-

eral hundred Sioux. There were seven passengers in
the coach, among them the division agent of the line.
All were well armed. Buffalo Bill's horses, though
he whipped them into full speed, were not as swift as
the Indian arrows, and the division agent was hit.
Several horses were wounded, but the stage kept on,
with the pasengers directing a hot fire against the
Indians until, upon reaching Three Crossings, they
were rescued by soldiers who drove back the braves.
In after years Buffalo Bill re-enacted this dramatic
scene in his Wild West show. On another occasion,
Buffalo Bill's stage was attacked by Indians, two
passengers were killed and another wounded before
he reached the safety of a station.

There were other drivers of picturesque name,
Rattlesnake Pete, Fiddler Jim, Happy Jack, Smiling
Tom, One-eyed Tom, Cross-eye John, Red Horse,
Rowdy Pete, Fish-creek Bill, and Long Slim. All of
these men were skilled drivers, as was Bob Hedges,
who acquired a reputation for playing "Get out of
the Wilderness" on his copper bugle as the coach
rolled into the station. He liked fast driving and was
reported to have driven a stage forty-eight miles in
one day.

Another driver gained special distinction because
of his bravery during an Indian attack. Bob Ridley
was taking an extra coach from Atchison to Denver.
In the Platte hills, just after he had passed Cottonwood Springs, he was attacked by a roving band of
Indians. For a distance of four miles along the level
road Ridley kept up a running fight, driving his team
at a gallop and shooting his revolver with telling

effect. Three braves were killed and ten wounded. Several Indian ponies were killed or crippled, and Ridley saved both coach and horses for the Holladay line. So pleased was the stagecoach owner with this brave performance that he presented Ridley with a fine gold watch.[71]

Every driver was a hero to the stock tender, whose greatest ambition was to please his superior by keeping the animals in excellent condition. The tenders were employed at all stations and drew a salary of forty to fifty dollars a month. The life of the tender employed at the swing station was lonely indeed. His only entertainment was the reading of old magazines and papers. When the stages stopped at his station he is said to have offered anywhere from twenty-five cents to one dollar each for copies of *Harper's Weekly, Leslie's Weekly,* a late newspaper, or a yellow-backed novel. One tender, described by a passenger as unkempt and sunburned, offered a dollar for any paper under ten days old; he had not seen a newspaper for one long week. Other visitors came to the swing stations: the division blacksmith, whose salary varied from one hundred to one hundred twenty-five dollars monthly; harness makers and repairers, who drew the same salary; and carpenters, whose pay was seventy-five dollars a month. The coach repairers usually worked only at division centers.[72]

[71] Dawson scrap-book (Library of Colorado state historical society), IV, 107; Barnes, *op. cit.,* 30; Root and Connelley, *op. cit.,* 271, 275, 277, 464; Kansas scrap-book (Library of Kansas state historical society), II, 41.

[72] *Ibid.,* 72, 76; Richardson, *Beyond the Mississippi,* 331; Barnes, *op. cit.,* 72, 97; Coman, *Economic beginnings of the far west,* 357; Rusling, *Great west,* 207.

The messenger, although not so spectacular as the driver, was fully as important an employee of the stage line. His was a responsible position. Acting as a stage conductor, he worked in a division of two hundred to two hundred and fifty miles and was paid sixty-one and a half dollars a month and board. Seated beside the driver, armed and on the lookout for outlaws or road agents, he guarded the treasure and packages of the coach. For nine days out of every three weeks he rested in order that he might be alert for his run. Then for from six days and nights he kept his nerve-wracking vigil. As mining operations increased in the west the value of the stage's cargo increased, and also the desperados. Some of these were disgruntled former employees of the stage company. Under these circumstances it was extremely necessary to hire level-headed messengers who could be trusted. It became a further responsibility to guard the heavily armed express coaches on the line. As the hauling of express grew in importance it was decided to send out a special coach on mondays which would carry no passengers. Atchison was doing much shipping to the west during 1864, especially to Central City and Black Hawk, Colorado territory. In july of that year Holladay bought three specially-built Concord express-wagons from the Abbot-Downing company of Concord, New Hampshire, for use on the line between Atchison and Denver.[73]

Express rates were high, one dollar a pound until

[73] *Rocky mountain news* (Denver), july 1, 1864; Ghent, *Road to Oregon*, 208, 209; Root and Connelley, *Overland stage*, 44, 69, 73, 537; Dawson scrap-book (Library of Colorado state historical society), XIV, 181. No mail from the east came to Atchison on monday.

1866, when they were reduced; and values of packages varied from a few dollars to several hundred dollars, with charges from seventy-five cents to one hundred and fifty dollars. There was a great rivalry among the express companies for a share of the Holladay business. Before 1866 the United States Express company handled the greatest number of packages on the Holladay line. By 1866, however, Holladay was handling his own express business. By this time there were mining developments in Montana and Idaho territories and much express was being shipped from the mines to Salt Lake City and to Denver, Atchison, and other eastern points. A large amount of express was also sent to Salt Lake City from points farther west. The rival express companies, the American, United States, and Wells, Fargo tried various means of persuasion on Holladay to get a share of this increased business, but all their efforts were unsuccessful.

Gold dust, bullion, coin, and bank treasury notes were not allowed to go as baggage. After december 10, 1864, gold dust, bullion, and treasure were carried by express-coach from Central City to Atchison in all sums of one hundred dollars, or in greater amounts than one hundred dollars, at one and one-half per cent of the currency value. The same rate was charged for the transportation of treasure from Atchison to Central City. In 1865 Holladay concluded an arrangement with the United States Express company and the American Express company for the transportation of express freight and treasure from New York at reduced rates. Currency and gold were carried in 1865 from Atchison to Denver at one and one-half per cent, and express was freighted between the same cities for fifty cents a pound.

Holladay's concern with gold mining led to an interest in financial securities. He became a banking associate of W. L. Halsey of Salt Lake City. On may 4, 1865 the Camp Douglas *Daily Union Vedette,* carried the following advertisement:

BEN HOLLADAY   W. L. HALSEY
NEW YORK   G.S.L. CITY

Holladay & Halsey
Bankers

At the office of the Overland Stage line, Great Salt Lake City, will pay the highest rates for gold dust and coin. Dust bought for coin or currency.

Cash paid for government vouchers. Drafts payable in coin or currency sold on New York, San Francisco, California, Virginia City, Idaho, Denver City, Colorado, Atchison, Kansas, Portland, Oregon, and Victoria, British Columbia.

Postage currency and revenue stamps for sale.[74]

In spite of the widening of his interests Holladay attended to the smallest concern of his employees. He bought clothing for his men in the east; overcoats of Irish frieze lined with blue shaker flannel, cut long, with capes that reached to the hands, high-topped boots, and warm underclothing. These were distributed along the express line and issued to the men. Each employee took whatever he needed and

---

[74] U.S. Senate. *Miscellaneous documents,* 46 cong., 2 sess., I, no. 19, 84; Black Hawk (Colo. terr.) *mining journal,* december 10, 1864; Atchison (Kans.) *daily free press,* september 7, 1865; Root and Connelley, *Overland stage,* 64; Camp Douglas (Utah terr.) *daily union vedette,* may 4, 1865.

had it charged to his account with the company. Holladay made no profit on the deal, as the men paid only the cost of the material and transportation.[75]

The upkeep of stages was also Holladay's concern. He used about one hundred and ten coaches in regular transportation. Made by the Abbot-Downing company of Concord, New Hampshire, they were the best of their type. When new they cost from one thousand to fifteen hundred dollars. Holladay replaced the worn coaches with new ones, adding twenty-nine in 1864, twelve in 1865, and two in 1866.

The stagecoaches bought by Holladay in 1864 weighed about a ton. Sand boxes were placed beneath the coach where the sand could be dropped upon the brake sticks when necessary. The brake sticks were three to four inches wide, making it possible for the driver to put great resistance upon the moving wheels. Each coach had side lights and large candle lamps for the interior.[76] The average coach seated nine passengers on the three inside seats, and, if the coach carried an extra seat behind the driver, from five to seven on top. Passengers usually preferred the inside back seat with its large head-rest. Late-comers drew the middle seat which had no back. Some of the Holladay coaches in 1865 were built to carry seventeen passengers, with an extra seat over the boot, the tri-

[75] Coutant, *History of Wyoming*, I, 369. A writer in the *Idaho daily statesman* (Boise), october 21, 1923, wrote that each suit and each overcoat cost $45.

[76] Burgum, letter to author, I, 2, MS.; Atchison (Kans.) *daily free press*, may 17, 1865; Rusling, *Across America*, 40; Root and Connelley, *Overland stage*, 76, 540; U.S. Senate. *Report*, 44 cong., 2 sess., no. 583, 1; *Miscellaneous documents*, 46 cong., 2 sess., I, no. 19, 87.

angular "tail" of the coach, and one behind the driver. These were hauled by six horses or mules.[77]

A part of the driver's work was to grease the stage at each home station. This work was called "doping," and if the driver forgot to dope his wheels a "hot box" resulted. During the summer of 1863 a coach developed a hot box while on the road. At the next station it was found that a spindle was cutting. The remedy for the situation was grease, but there was no grease to be found. The driver was about to wrap grass around the spindle and risk the journey to the next station when a resourceful passenger drew forth a sack containing some cheese. The driver, equal to any emergency, sliced the cheese and applied it to the wheel, which responded at once to the treatment and carried coach and passengers without mishap to the next station.

The wheels of the coach were heavy, with wide thick tires. Its strong body, built of white oak, was braced with iron bands and slung upon stout leather thorough-braces. There were adjustable leather curtains designed to keep out wind, rain, snow, and dust, but from early accounts of stage passengers it would seem that these were never completely efficient. The box holding treasure and express was placed beneath the driver's seat, while the passengers' baggage was carried in the boot. Passengers were allowed twenty-five pounds of baggage free of charge, with excess at one dollar a pound. Mail sacks were also carried in the boot, except when there was an overflow, and then

77 Root and Connelley, *op. cit.,* 48; Birge, *Awakening of the desert,* 409; Atchison (Kans.) *daily free press,* may 17, 1865; Rusling, *Great west,* 41.

they were thrown upon the floor of the coach to slide about, much to the discomfiture of the passengers.

Despite its drawbacks, the overland coach, with its brilliant red body striped with black and its straw-colored chassis, was an impressive sight as it pulled into the stage stations, drawn by its lively animals and accompanied by much fanfare. Until april 1866 the name OVERLAND STAGE LINE was conspicuous on the coaches. After this the name was changed to HOLLA-DAY O.M. & EX. CO.

Holladay made frequent trips over the line in his private coach, said to have cost several thousand dollars. This special de luxe model had cushioned seats and was mounted on spiral springs, so even his wife, who was not strong, could make the journey without too much discomfort. The interior was equipped with expensive side curtains, beautiful lamps with silver cases, and a writing table. On tour it was followed closely by another coach carrying a cook and servants, as well as supplies of necessities and luxuries for the trip, such as special mattresses, brandy, and cigars. Each coach was drawn by six horses, and the whole gave an impression of importance in keeping with the position of a stagecoach king.

Other out-of-the-ordinary coaches sometimes appeared on the line. A double-decked omnibus ran for a time on the Denver–Missouri City route, and mud-wagons were used in the rough mountainous country. These were covered with cloth and built low in order to lessen the danger of overturning. Nine passengers were accommodated inside and one on the outside seat with the driver. During some seasons of the year the mud-wagons were used on the Denver–North Platte road.[78]

The discomforts endured by passengers in stage-coach days were many. Rain and dust came in through the ill-fitting curtains. The jolting was so intense that after several days of riding there was much complaint about bone-aches and sore flesh. To divert themselves from their bodily pains, the passengers talked, and when conversation was exhausted they sang familiar songs. The strains of "Georgia," "John Brown," and "Rally Round the Flag" out on the western prairie, far from the scene of battle, reminded them that a war was going on, and possibly that there were worse discomforts than those they were at the moment experiencing.

The nerve strain was perhaps more severe than the jolts. The more seasoned passenger kept a calm silence as the coach tipped toward the edge of a precipice; others were not so unconcerned when looking down into several hundred feet of chasm. Narrow, hazardous canyons were sometimes driven through at great speed, although the best drivers, sure of the road and their animals, were not so reckless as they appeared. There were fewer dangers, from the standpoint of driving, on the plains than in the mountains, but sometimes a heavy hailstorm would frighten the horses or mules into running away, and then the pas-

---

[78] *Ibid.*, 148, 149; Paxson, *Last American frontier,* 178, 179; Kansas scrap-book (Library of Kansas state historical society), VIII, 138; Denver *times,* december 6, 1915; Ware, *Indian war of 1864,* 423; Dawson scrap-book (Library of Colorado state historical society), XIV, 132; U.S. Senate. *Miscellaneous documents,* 46 cong., 2 sess., I, no. 19, 69; Twombly, interview with author, I, MS.; *Rocky mountain news* (Denver), march 28, 1863.

sengers were obliged to hold on frantically. On the
plains, too, there was the tension of Indian fear,
which never for a moment let the traveler relax completely.

· Occasionally one of the group would become suddenly ill. He would be obliged to drink either brack-
ish water or bad whisky, unless of course he had come
prepared for any emergency. Others drank the whisky
to ease throats clogged with alkaline dust and sometimes became drunk enough to create excitement. In
march 1866 a passenger became insane and tried to
kill his fellow passengers. The stage was rolling along
the plains of western Nebraska territory with its
seven occupants when the madman became violent.
He stabbed one man several times, killed another
with a pistol, and injured a third. He was finally shot
and mortally wounded.

Even when all was comparatively peaceful within
the coach, rest was "a poor apology for tired nature's
sweet restorer," according to one who had attempted
to sleep going overland. Passengers, dozing in corners
or curled up on the middle seat, would fall in a heap
at a sudden lurch, untangle themselves, and doze off
again. Often they resorted to borrowing hay from a
station, putting it on the top of the coach, and cover-
ing it with blankets for a bed. Then they would insure
themselves against waking up on the prairie by tying
ropes around their bodies and fastening them to the
railings. Such a bed was greatly preferable to the
sardine-pack inside, especially in warm seasons. Cool
nights, however, numbed the muscles, and passengers
would often waken stiff and ill-tempered, and people

grew so careless in their dress that a fellow passenger reported of such a scene, "everybody's back hair comes down, and what is nature and what is art in costume and character is revealed." [79]

More has been written of the stagecoach and its passengers than of the faithful animals pulling their heavy load through every extremity of weather and altitude. Seventeen hundred mules and horses were in use on the Holladay line. Holladay instructed his stock buyers to select only the best of livestock and insisted that they be well cared for. The animals varied in weight. Of the six-horse strings, the team nearest the coach, called wheel-horses or wheel-mules on the plains, was the heaviest, weighing usually from one thousand to twelve hundred pounds. In the mountains the wheel-horses were called tongue-horses or tongue-mules. On the Julesburg to Denver division the road was at places so deep in sand that heavy mules were needed.[80] Teams were matched in color, the bay and brown animals predominating, although Holladay had some gray and white teams. On the Georgetown division in Colorado territory six snow-white horses hauled the brilliant coach. Although this was considered the most beautiful team on the line, the Benham mules which worked from Denver were reported to be the fastest. It had a rival in the "cat-fish" group of dapple grays. This team established a record of fifteen miles in fifty-five minutes on the

79 Ibid., march 28, 1866; Rusling, Great west, 148-150; Barnes, From Atlantic to Pacific, 7, 8; Bowles, Our new west, 86, 201; Rusling, Across America, 44.

80 U.S. Senate. Report, 44 cong., 2 sess., no. 583, 1; Miscellaneous documents, 46 cong., 2 sess., I, no. 19, 69; Twombly, interview with author, I, 2, MS.

road from Denver to Golden. Another fast group of grays was the four-horse team driven by Buffalo Bill west of Fort Kearny.

The trotting teams often covered eight miles an hour and occasionally ten or twelve. Holladay had a reason for wanting fast livestock. They had to be able to outrun the Indian ponies if attacked, and an expensive live horse was cheaper in the long run than a cheap one full of arrows. It was good publicity, too, for the line, when the coach was wheeled into town at a spirited gallop.[81] So far famed were these speeding Holladay horses that they were even spoken of in the land of the Pharoahs. Mark Twain wrote of an American traveling in Egypt who, when told that Moses took forty years to lead the tribes of Israel three hundred miles from Egypt to the Promised Land, was not impressed. He had himself crossed the western desert to California in an overland stage. "Forty years?" he said, incredulously. "Only three hundred miles? Humph! Ben Holladay would have fetched them through in thirty-six hours." [82]

In the years between 1862 and 1865 the Civil war created a large demand for mules and horses, and Holladay was forced to pay a high price for his livestock. It is estimated that he invested five hundred thousand dollars in all for the livestock used in his stage business. Good horses were valued at one hundred seventy-five to two hundred fifty dollars, while ponies cost from fifty to one hundred dollars each.

81 *Ibid.;* Root and Connelley, *Overland stage,* 492, 493; Rusling, *Across America,* 41, 42; Rusling, *Great west,* 42.

82 Clemens, *Roughing it,* 42.

Mules were priced at one hundred to two hundred dollars. The oxen used in freighting for the stage line also brought a high price. In july 1865 oxen sold at Atchison for one hundred sixty to one hundred seventy dollars a yoke, while later the price rose to one hundred seventy-five and two hundred dollars. On one occasion United States soldiers at Fort Kearny confiscated twenty-nine yoke of Holladay's oxen for their own use. Cattle were valued at fifty to seventy-five dollars each. During the serious Indian depredations of 1862 and 1864 Holladay was forced to replace many animals. Nevertheless, he continued to buy good livestock because he believed it sound economy.[83]

To prove the superiority of his fast livestock Holladay once bet his attorney, General Bela Hughes, that he could travel faster over his route than steamers could go from coast to coast. He prepared carefully for the race, sending word ahead for all stations to have their best teams in readiness. The entire system was upset and agog. On the trip between Salt Lake City and Denver, Holladay was accompanied by General P. E. Connor, commander of Camp Douglas. The stage line owner appeared at the Denver stage office wearing a good-looking sombrero and puffing the usual long black cigar. Bob Spotswood, a Holladay official, had the famous Benham team in readiness to drive them from Denver to Julesburg. At the end of the first run, the speedy mules were replaced by the "catfish" team of dapple grays, which upheld

---

[83] U.S. Senate. *Miscellaneous documents,* 46 cong., 2 sess., I, no. 19, 30, 39, 87; *Report,* 46 cong., 2 sess., I, no. 216, 12-18; Atchison (Kans.) *daily free press,* july 8, 1865.

its reputation for speed by traveling the next eleven miles in fifty-five minutes. The distance from Denver to Julesburg was covered in twenty hours. The stage came reeling into Julesburg at such a rate of speed that Connor's negro servant all but turned white with fear. Holladay himself was impressed, and is reported to have turned to Spotswood saying, "My son, you've done well. How many mules do you suppose I've killed?" At whatever cost, he had won his bet by making the trip from Salt Lake City to Atchison in eight days and six hours, and had advertised his stage line over the nation.[84]

A racing team, especially in mountainous country, must have a good set of harness. Holladay never took a chance with anything but the best. Usually this was the "Hill" brand, bought at Concord, New Hampshire. The cost was one hundred ten to one hundred fifty dollars for one four-horse set, with five dollars a set additional cost for transportation. Holladay spent at least fifty-five thousand dollars for harness.[85]

Equipment was necessary for the auxiliary business of freighting. Freight, wood, and feed for the livestock had to be hauled. In 1864, Holladay hired fifteen thousand men, twenty thousand wagons, and one hundred fifty thousand animals for the transporting of one hundred million pounds of freight between the Missouri river and the Rocky mountains. As freight charges were seventeen cents a pound for each

[84] Dawson scrap-book (Library of Colorado state historical society), XIV, 115.

[85] Coutant, *History of Wyoming*, I, 388; Root and Connelley, *Overland stage*, 74; U.S. Senate. *Miscellaneous documents*, 46 cong., 2 sess., I, no. 19, 30, 49.

one hundred miles, there was a profit in the business
for the contractor. The "J. Murphywagon" made in
St. Louis, carrying three tons of freight, was commonly used on the Holladay lines. Grain was usually
hauled from Salt Lake City or Atchison, but in times
of scarcity could be secured at Denver or St. Louis.
Holladay regularly used six thousand horses and
mules for all types of work. These were increased, in
times of Indian troubles, when stations, food, fuel,
grain, and other property were destroyed and had to
be replaced as soon as possible in order that service
might be resumed.[86]

The need for a large amount of equipment can be
understood when it is remembered that the Holladay
stage lines were about thirty-three hundred miles
long. At the time of their greatest extension they went
from Atchison to Salt Lake City and from there to
Boise City, Idaho territory and to Virginia City,
Montana territory; also from Denver to Central City,
from Nebraska City to Fort Kearny, and from
Omaha to Fort Kearny.

The main line started at Atchison and ran northwest about one hundred miles to Marysville, Kansas.
The road then crossed the Little Blue river and continued northwest along its course. It crossed the di-
vide into the Platte valley, going through Fort
Kearny, Nebraska territory, to Plum Creek, Julesburg, and Denver. From Denver it went northwest
to Boulder creek, to Laporte on the Cache la Poudre,

86 Coutant, *op. cit.,* I, 388, 389; Rusling, *Great west,* 40; Root and Connelley, *op. cit.,* 72; Nebraska state historical society *collections,* XVI, 57;
Hulbert, *Paths of inland commerce,* 190.

COMMERCIAL STREET, ATCHISON, 1866
From a contemporary drawing by William M. Merrick

Julesburg, where the stagecoaches crossed the
Platte river, was an important home station. In 1865
its buildings, the largest on the line between Fort
Kearny and Denver, were valued at ten thousand dollars. There were twelve in all, including the home
station, the stable, blacksmith shop, store, telegraph
office, and outbuildings. Three were frame buildings,
but the rest were of cedar logs which had been hauled
by oxen from Cottonwood Springs, one hundred and
five miles away. Freight trade brought the town much
wealth. In 1864 freight wagons to the number of 3574
arrived at Julesburg; 28,592 horses and 4258 men
were employed.[103]

Julesburg was named for an old French trader.
Jules had worked for Holladay for a short time as
agent, until it was discovered that he was robbing the
company and letting others loot the line. Holladay
sent Slade, then in good repute, to replace Jules and
to clean up the division. Slade had already effectively
decreased the number of outlaws in that region, and
was reported to have killed twenty of them. Jules resented Slade's arrival and at his first opportunity,
when the two met at the general store, fired the con-
tents of a double-barreled shotgun at Slade and left
him lying on the floor for dead. But the sturdy Slade
was not so easily disposed of; he merely lay in bed for
several weeks, recuperating and planning his revenge.
Differing versions of the finale of this affair have
been propounded. It is said that either Slade or his

---

[103] Root and Connelley, *Overland stage,* 64, 215; Nebraska state historical society *collections,* XVI, 56; U.S. Senate. *Miscellaneous documents,*
46 cong., 2 sess., I, no. 19, 71.

friends caught the fleeing Frenchman north of Julesburg, brought him back to the station, and tied him
to a post in a corral. Some reports say that Jules was
shot and killed on the spot, while others have it that
he was finally allowed to leave the region alive, after
being given a severe punishment. A further em-
bellishment to the story says that Slade cut off old
Jules's ears and kept them for a souvenir.

Julesburg acquired such a bad reputation that
Holladay changed its name to Overland City and
gave it that official name on the stage line schedule.
However, its old name remained a favorite with passengers and employees.[104]

Denver had been an important settlement from its
beginning and continued to grow. It was more sub-
stantially built than St. Joseph or Atchison. In 1863,
claiming a population of five thousand people, it had
five brick stores, four churches, a school, a United
States mint, two banks, two theaters, three daily newspapers, and many gambling houses. At this time the
Holladay stage station was at the Planter's hotel, but
three years later it was transferred to a two-story
brick building.[105]

The cost of building stations varied according to
their nearness to timber. Between Fort Kearny and
Denver, and also between Salt Lake City and a point
fifty miles west of Denver, there was a scarcity of
timber. According to an estimate by General Hughes,
home stations between Julesburg and Denver cost at

104 *Ibid.;* Dawson scrap-book (Library of Colorado state historical
society), XIV, 181; Root and Connelley, *op. cit.,* 215.

105 *Ibid.,* 164; Barnes, *From Atlantic to Pacific,* 29; Barber and Howe,
All the western states, 518.

least three thousand dollars each, and Elkhorn station east of Fort Kearny was valued at two to three thousand dollars.

Life at the home stations was less monotonous than at the swing stations. In addition to the daily arrival and departure of coaches there was the social life of the people who made it their home. When a dance was held at a home station, men and women would come from as far away as fifty miles, by stagecoach or wagon and often on horseback. Music for the dances at Fort Bridger was enhanced by the novelty of a piano which had been hauled from New York twenty-five hundred miles, and for half of that distance by ox-cart.[106]

At the twenty-five stations between Atchison and Denver there was great variation in the kind and quality of meals. Besides the constant differences in climate, soil, and personnel, there was the still greater variation according to the year and month. During the time of Indian raids all foods were alarmingly scarce. Although there was less variety otherwise in the winter months, there were many more kinds of meat than we have today in our best dining-cars and restaurants. Beef, ham, bear, trout, buffalo, antelope, turkey, elk, deer, salt pork, bacon, and chicken were served at various seasons, as well as fresh vegetables, eggs, butter, milk, cream, canned and dried fruits, brown sugar, pies, pickles, bread and saleratus biscuit, tea, and coffee.

Although complaints against the food were com-

---

[106] Coutant, *History of Wyoming*, I, 388; Richardson, *Beyond the Mississippi*, 343; Root and Connelley, *Overland stage*, 67, 93, 94.

mon, praise was often given where it was due. Holladay, on his numerous trips over the line, found a
favorite eating place. At Thirty-two-mile Creek, Mrs.
Emery, the cook, always provided an appetizing
breakfast, and for Holladay she did her best. After
one particularly delicious breakfast of fried bacon,
corn dodgers, and coffee, Holladay tossed her a
twenty-dollar gold piece and told her to keep the
change.

Travelers often carried their own food with them,
frequently something offensive to their fellow passengers, such as cheese, crackers, herring, and bologna.
Others depended upon what the station might provide. There was always greater variety in the stations
near division centers, while at the more distant stations fresh vegetables, fruits, and milk were scarce
and the travelers were forced to be satisfied with thin
coffee, fried salt pork, and saleratus biscuits. Holladay made a constant effort to improve the quality of
the food during his years as manager of the stage line,
but certain conditions were beyond his control.

The price of meals on the main line varied from
fifty cents to two dollars, the lower prices prevailing
in the eastern division. During the fall of 1863 food
prices were high, and meals accordingly higher. At
Latham eggs were one dollar and a quarter to one
dollar and a half a dozen, butter and coffee one dollar
a pound.[107]

As variable as the food prices were the ticket prices.

107 *Ibid.*, 87, 94-97, 332; Bowles, *Our new west*, 38; Twombly, interview with author, 1, 2, MS.; Dawson scrap-book (Library of Colorado
state historical society), XIV, 115; Kansas scrap-book (Library of Kansas
state historical society), VIII, H, 138; Rusling, *Great west*, 42, 143, 149.

Because of the great expense of operation (over two million dollars a year) and the limited capacity of the coaches, these were necessarily high. The rates differed between 1862 and 1866 because of varying costs of operation and values of gold and currency during the war. It is noticeable that Holladay reduced his rates in 1866 when the Indian menace had been practically removed. The following table illustrates:

FROM ATCHISON

	1862	1863	1864	1865	1866
To Denver	$75	$75		$175	$175–$125
To Salt Lake City	150	150		350	250–225
To Virginia City					350–330
To Placerville	225	225	200	450–500	

The fare from Atchison to Denver underwent other changes. In june 1863 it was raised from $75 to $125; on august 11, 1865 it was reduced from $175 to $100, but raised again on august 22 to $150.

The fare from Boise City to Helena City (Montana territory) in 1865 was $145. Boise City was in Idaho territory while Helena City was about one hundred miles from Virginia City, Montana territory. In the latter part of 1866, the eastern terminus of the main line was Fort Kearny because the Union Pacific railroad was completed from Omaha to that station. The fare at that time from Fort Kearny was $450 to Nevada, $500 to California, and about $500 to points in Idaho and Montana territories. Rusling wrote that fares in 1866 from Fort Kearny were $150 to Denver and $300 to Salt Lake City.

Way fares were also high. These varied from

twelve and one-half to fifteen cents a mile. A study of
the fare tables shows that in 1862 the stagecoach passenger paid a little less than nine cents a mile to travel
from Atchison to Denver and almost twelve cents a
mile to ride to California. The travel rates of 1862
remained in effect until may of the following year.
Holladay was then compelled to raise the rates because of losses from Indian depredations, and the
passengers paid about twenty-seven cents a mile to
go from Atchison to Denver. The same scale was in
effect in 1865.[108]

Changes in economic conditions affected the cost
of travel. In 1865 the price of gold had risen with the
currency depreciation, and in addition the stage lines
had suffered heavily during the Indian warfare of
the previous year. Consequently ticket prices rose.
Passengers were compelled to pay one dollar to one
dollar and fifty cents a pound for excess baggage.
Twenty-five pounds were allowed each passenger
without charge, provided it was not gold dust, bullion, coin, or bank or treasury notes. Passengers were
urged to send heavy baggage by ship to the western
coast by way of the isthmus of Panama.[109]

---

[108] *Ibid.*, 41; Kansas scrap-book (Library of Kansas state historical
society), VIII, H, 138; Rusling, *Across America*, 41; Ghent, *Road to Oregon*, 209; Kansas state historical society *collections*, III, bibliography;
Philatelic gossip, VIII, no. 11, 355; Bradley, *Pony express*, 161, 162; Root
and Connelley, *Overland stage*, 49; Atchison (Kans.) *daily free press*,
may 12, august 11, 1865; Rusling, *Great west*, 41; see also Munson,
"Pioneer life on American frontier," in *Journal of American history*, I,
no. 1, 102.

[109] Barnes, *From Atlantic to Pacific*, 21; Leavenworth (Kans.) *daily
conservative*, may 19, 1865; Atchison (Kans.) *daily free press*, august
11, 1865; Trails clippings (Library of Kansas state historical society),
II, no. 11, 10.

No matter how high a price the passenger might pay for his ticket, he was never certain of a prompt arrival at his destination. At such times as the coaches were free from attack by Indians or road agents they were often delayed by conditions of the weather. Sudden rains and spring thaws swelled the streams, and often the teams had to swim across them while the coaches, built in such a way as to keep an even balance, floated behind. Snow and flooding streams checked all mail from the east to Salt Lake City from march 23 to april 4, 1862. In december of the following year, the plains of Kansas and Nebraska territory were covered with deep snow and the cold was the worst in years. A severe snow-storm destroyed the mail road in february 1864. One coach was unable to travel more than eight miles from Salt Lake City and was obliged to return. During the next winter snow was from four to five feet deep in the Boise basin.[110]

Greater speed was attained and schedules were more regular between Atchison and Fort Kearny, where there were rolling prairies and only a slight upgrade, than from Fort Kearny to Denver, where the roads were sandy and sometimes steep, and Indian attacks were more frequent. The record runs were usually made on the prairie stretches. In the fall of 1863 a stage traveled the six hundred and fifty-three miles from Denver to Atchison in five days eight hours. This was an average of four and one-half miles an hour, with stops included. Another Holla-

[110] San Francisco *daily evening bulletin*, january 24, 1865; Kansas scrap-book (Library of Kansas state historical society), XII, 24; Walla Walla (Wash. terr.) *statesman*, february 3, 1865; *Philatelic gossip*, VIII, no. 11, 365.

day stage with twelve passengers and five hundred pounds of mail went from Big Sandy to Thompson's station in southern Nebraska territory, a distance of fourteen miles, in fifty-two minutes, traveling at an average speed of sixteen miles an hour.[111] In july 1865 a stage traveled the five hundred and thirty miles between Atchison and Julesburg in four days, five hours, and forty-five minutes. The schedule between Atchison and Salt Lake City was:

APRIL I TO NOVEMBER 30   243 HOURS

Leave Atchison daily, 8 a.m. Arrive Salt Lake City, 11th day by 11 a.m.

Leave Salt Lake City daily, 10 a.m. Arrive Atchison, 11th day by 1 p.m.

DECEMBER I TO MARCH 31   306 HOURS

Leave Atchison daily, 8 a.m. Arrive Salt Lake City, 14th day by 2 a.m.

Leave Salt Lake City daily, 7 p.m. Arrive Atchison, 14th day by 1 p.m.

One of the fastest runs on the line was made in 1865. Holladay, in San Francisco, had received a telegram calling him to New York. Orders were sent ahead at once to division agents to provide fresh relays of livestock, and Holladay hurried eastward by special coach. He traveled the two thousand miles to Atchison in twelve days and two hours, which was five days faster than the regular schedule. It was reported that the trip cost twenty thousand dollars in wear on coaches and livestock, but it was good publicity for Holladay and the overland line.[112]

111 Root and Connelley, *Overland stage*, 71-72.
112 Richardson, *Beyond the Mississippi*, 331; Bowles, *Across the continent*, 55.

Other famous coach trips were made in 1865. Speaker Schuyler Colfax, accompanied by Samuel Bowles, editor of the *Springfield* (Massachusetts) *Republican,* and Albert D. Richardson of the *Boston Journal* made the trip westward. The distance between Atchison and Denver was made in four and one-half days. In october of the same year the trip from Denver to Atchison was traveled in a still shorter time. A Holladay coach left Denver on october 18 at 7:46 p.m. and arrived at Atchison by 8:30 p.m. three days later, which meant a record of three days, eleven hours, and fifteen minutes for the trip. The road from Fort Kearny was covered in twenty-three hours, with a stop at Seneca of one hour and ten minutes. The run caused much surprised admiration, and it was boasted that Holladay's coaches were almost as fast as the railroad train.[113]

Comparisons between the divisions were inevitable. The division from Salt Lake City to Green River was considered to have better livestock and coaches than the road from Denver to Green River, and drivers on the western unit were believed to be more courteous than those on the eastern part of the run. The line from Denver to Atchison had a reputation for its tactful employees, fine livestock, and modern coaches.[114]

It was especially urgent that a regular schedule be kept by the stage line because Holladay's mail contract depended upon prompt and safe delivery of the mails. He had taken over the old contracts of Russell, Majors, and Waddell in 1862, which were to expire

---

[113] *Ibid.,* 10, 12, 20; *Missouri historical review,* xxv, 364.

[114] Sacramento *daily union,* january 20, 1864.

on june 30, two years later. During the spring, although Holladay had attempted to secure renewals and additional contracts, there was some anxiety as to whether or not the contracts would be renewed. Previous to this time the postal department had sent out a special postal agent, C. M. Carter, to inspect the Overland route. Carter reported that bridges and ferries were lacking between Atchison and Salt Lake City and that swollen rivers were delaying the mails. However, Postmaster-general Montgomery Blair recommended a renewal of the contract, and a bill for that purpose was introduced in the senate. Its passage was blocked by Senator John Conness of California. Conness was a bitter enemy of Louis McLane, who was associated with the Wells, Fargo Express company. The Wells, Fargo company was a heavy investor in the Overland Mail company which carried the mail to California from Salt Lake City.[115]

The postmaster-general advertised in october 1863 for bids to be received at the mail contract office for the transportation of United States mail on certain routes in Kansas and the territories of Colorado, Utah, and Nevada. Bids were to be for two or four years of service, to be submitted on march 3, 1864. On january 21, 1864, and on march 22 of that year, Blair again advertised for bids. It was not until advertisement number five was printed and given to the public that Holladay submitted a bid.

The contract on route 14260 called for service between Atchison, Kansas or St. Joseph, Missouri, and Salt Lake City, Utah territory. The contractor was

115 San Francisco *daily evening bulletin,* february 9, 1863, june 7, 16, 1864.

required to furnish daily service in each direction on the route and to supply any intermediate offices between the termini of the line. The contract was to run from october 1, 1864, to september 30, 1868, inclusive. It required the contractor to give eleven-day service during the eight months of the year from april 1 to december 1, and fourteen-day service during the other four months.[116]

Bids were to be received to extend the daily service from Salt Lake City to Virginia City, Nevada territory, and to Folsom, California, where the new mining activities necessitated mail delivery. The successful bidder was to furnish daily service to Denver by the most direct route from the main line, and if possible to start service on july 1, 1864. He was required to transport all through letter mails, all local and way mails, also all mail matter prepaid at letter rates. He was not, however, compelled to handle document and paper mail to the Pacific coast, as the postal department had contracted, for one hundred and sixty thousand dollars a year, to have such mail carried by steamship.

Holladay had several rival bidders for the contract. Bids for the service between Atchison and Salt Lake City ranged from one of three hundred seventy-five thousand dollars by Joseph Burbank to Holladay's bid of three hundred eighty-five thousand dollars. John A. Heistand bid seven hundred fifty thousand dollars, Holladay eight hundred twenty

---

[116] Postmaster-general's *report*, 1864, in U.S. House. *Executive documents*, 38 cong., 2 sess., V, no. 1, 782; VIII, no. 24, 1-6, 10-12. The postmaster-general reserved the right to name either Atchison or St. Joseph for the eastern terminus.

thousand dollars, and the Overland Mail company eight hundred eighty thousand dollars for the contract to carry all mail between Folsom and Atchison. The time limit for acceptance of bids expired at three in the afternoon on june 14, 1864, and the contract was awarded to Heistand as the lowest bidder.

On june 16 George W. McLellan, second assistant postmaster-general, informed Heistand by letter that his low bid had been accepted. McLellan asked Heistand to send the contract and to prepare to commence service by october 1. On the same date Heistand telegraphed Blair that he wished to withdraw his offer as conditions had arisen which would prevent his fulfilling the contract. Holladay also on that date, june 16, 1864, wrote a letter to the postmaster-general informing him that Heistand, having withdrawn his bid, stood as a failing bidder or no bidder at all, and that Holladay himself was legally and justly entitled to the contract at his own bid of eight hundred twenty thousand dollars. He said, further, that the congressional law of july 2, 1836, section twenty-four, and that of march 3, 1845, section eighteen, required the postal department to award contracts to the lowest bidder, provided that he had not failed on a previous contract and could furnish satisfactory guarantees.

Holladay's letter presented difficulties, as the house of representatives had passed a resolution to secure information from Blair concerning the recent Overland contract, and the senate had appointed a committee to consider the resolution. Blair wrote to Senator S. C. Pomeroy of the senate committee, submitting

Holladay's letter. He explained that he wished to await the decision of the committee, reserving his own opinion on the legal point raised by Holladay until congress had taken action. The awarding of a contract to the rightful bidder became increasingly complicated when Heistand wrote to the postmaster-general on june 21. Heistand mentioned having received McLellan's letter announcing that as low bidder he had been awarded the contract, and said that he was now ready to execute the necessary bonds to carry out the contract. On june 22 Holladay added to the confusion by sending Blair a telegram informing him that, since Heistand's bid had once been withdrawn and could not legally be offered again, he himself had arranged to carry the United States mail.

Fortunately Blair had arranged with the old contractors to continue service until september 30, 1864. It would have been impossible for new carriers to establish their stations and have their livestock and other equipment along the line between june 22 and july 1. The arrangement, however, gave the impression that Holladay had been awarded the contract for another four years, and one hothead wrote to a Denver newspaper in protest. "For four years more," he said, "Colorado, Utah, and Nevada belong to Ben Holladay for a footstool, and may the Lord have mercy on them!" [117]

[117] U.S. House. *Executive documents,* 38 cong., 2 sess., VIII, no. 24, 12, 14-18, 20, 21; *Rocky mountain news* (Denver), june 30, 1864; Postmaster-general's *report,* 1864, 783. Congress had passed a resolution on march 25, 1864 to instruct the postmaster-general to send all paper and document mail by sea; Burbank bid $824,000 for service to Folsom and the Overland Mail company $384,000 for service between Salt Lake City and Atchison.

On july 15 Heistand wrote Blair that he understood he was to be released from his bid, since congress had passed a resolution giving the postmaster-general the right to negotiate with other bidders. Heistand's guarantors had suggested that they wished to be released, and now he himself was willing to withdraw from the field of bidders. This withdrawal improved the situation for a time. In july the head of the postal department ordered McLellan to offer Holladay the contract to carry the mail on route 10773 from Atchison or St. Joseph to Folsom City, California. On july 25 McLellan wrote Heistand that Blair had released him from his bid, and the matter was closed.

The offer made to Holladay was for seven hundred fifty thousand dollars a year from october 1, 1864, to june 30, 1868. It stipulated, however, that as the Pacific Railroad lengthened its lines the mail route should be decreased. In 1862 the Pacific Railroad bill had been passed by congress, and although active organization had scarcely begun two years later, the inevitable day of railroad domination was already beginning to cast its shadow over the stagecoach business. Holladay did not want the contract under such terms, and replied to the offer on july 18 saying that he could not accept it.

The postmaster-general now decided to drop Holladay from the field of bidders. He asked McLellan to telegraph Joseph H. Burbank of Falls City, Nebraska territory, that he had been awarded the overland mail contract for seven hundred fifty thousand dollars a year from october 1, 1864 to june 30,

1868. McLellan obeyed instructions and also sent full details of the contract to Burbank in a letter on july 20. When no answer had come from Burbank by july 30, Postmaster-general Blair telegraphed a second offer to the Nebraskan. On july 29 Burbank sent word to the second assistant postmaster-general that he had received the telegram and letter on july 27. "The proposition is accepted," Burbank said. "I await a reply at White Cloud, Kansas, before preparing for service." The postmaster-general delayed action on the offer. In the meantime Holladay, who had refused his offer of a contract because under its terms he would suffer a gradual diminution of pay as the length of his stage line was curtailed, thought the matter over more carefully. On august 5 he telegraphed from Saratoga, New York, that he would accept the contract at Heistand's bid. The following day he again telegraphed that he would accept the contract. On august 6 McLellan sent word to Holladay that Blair was pleased to hear of his acceptance and wished to see him in Washington within a week so that he could sign the necessary papers.

Whatever judgment may have been passed upon Blair's decision or upon Holladay's determination to get a favorable contract, one thing is evident, the postmaster-general was satisfied with the contractor's past service and felt it wiser to reemploy him than to give the contract to a new bidder.

Holladay wrote McLellan on august 6 asking the postal department to draw up two contracts for the overland route. He had arranged with the Overland Mail company to carry the mail between Salt Lake

City and Folsom, and he asked that one contract should be in his name for three hundred sixty-five thousand dollars while the other was to be for three hundred eighty-five thousand dollars in the name of W. B. Dinsmore, president of the Overland Mail company. The two amounted to seven hundred fifty thousand dollars. Blair was glad to have Holladay's acceptance and the contracts were drawn as he had requested.

After the business with Holladay and Dinsmore had been settled, Burbank made a final attempt to block the arrangement. On august 20 he sent a letter from Falls City to Blair, complaining of his failure to receive the contract after his bid had been accepted. He reminded Blair that he had telegraphed his acceptance of the offer, and said that his agent, who had been sent to Washington to execute the contract, had learned that one had been given to Holladay instead of to him. Blair's books, he said, did not show that Holladay had been given the contract on the day mentioned by Blair. Burbank demanded a full explanation of the matter, then added that he would still take the contract at seven hundred fifty thousand dollars a year if given four months in which to prepare for service. By this time, however, the contract had been executed, and that was the end of the matter.[118]

A. A. Selover and George Denison, who had been Holladay's friends for several years, acted as sureties for him. The contract required him to furnish daily service between Atchison and Salt Lake City, carry-

118 Postmaster-general's *report*, 1864, 782, 783; U.S. House. *Executive documents*, 38 cong., 2 sess., VIII, no. 24, 21-25; U.S. Senate. *Executive documents*, 46 cong., 2 sess., V, no. 211, 8, 9, 10.

ing the mails to these cities, to all intermediate offices on the line, and also to Denver by a direct branch from the main route. The requirements for handling the mail in a dependable manner stipulated that it was to be carried securely and safe from dampness, under oilcloth or bearskin when taken by horse, or in the boot of a stage, or under the driver's seat of a stage or any other vehicle. The contractor was held responsible for the action of the agents who carried the mail and could hire no employees under sixteen years of age. The contract provided that the carrier be paid quarterly for his services, in february, may, august, and november. He was to forfeit any pay for failure to make a scheduled trip, for violations of the rules, and for late schedules. It is doubtful if Holladay ever suffered any forfeits for infringements of the contract.

Holladay has been credited with the holding of nine mail contracts between 1862 and 1868. One agreement, however, was between the United States government and the Wells, Fargo company. This was for a contract from june 15, 1868, to september 30 of that year. Although the contract bore the name of Ben Holladay, he had sold out to the Wells, Fargo company in 1866. In another contract, number 15022, Holladay sublet the mail transportation between Boise City and The Dalles. The contracts varied in amounts from eighteen hundred forty-two dollars for six months' service to seven hundred fifty thousand dollars for a year. Of the latter, he sublet a part amounting to three hundred eighty-five thousand dollars.[119]

119 *Ibid.*, v, no. 211, 1. Holladay's mail contracts are listed in the appendix.

During the period in which his stagecoaches carried the mails Holladay received almost two million dollars, yet this amount scarcely paid the costs of operation for a single year. It was from the passenger and express business that he expected a profit during the four and one-half years of service. For the times and conditions under which he operated, Holladay carried on a large passenger and express business. It has been impossible to secure exact records of receipts from passengers and express on the Holladay lines, since the records were destroyed at the time of the San Francisco earthquake in 1906 when the Wells, Fargo offices were burned. The United States postal department does not give any information on the postal receipts from the Holladay lines. Receipts were often from one hundred fifty thousand to two hundred thousand dollars a month. The Atchison office did a thriving business at certain seasons of the year. On some days two thousand dollars were received from passenger fares, with additional returns on excess baggage at one dollar a pound adding to the income.[120]

At times of good passenger business it was not always possible to accommodate all who wished to make the trip on the Holladay lines. In 1864, when Denver was on a branch line, the main line being from Latham to Laporte, Denver passengers complained that they were unable to secure seats in the main line coaches. In a newspaper editorial it was said that the Overland Stage line was unequal to the demand made

---

[120] Root and Connelley, *Overland stage,* 488; Kansas scrap-book (Library of Kansas state historical society) VIII, H, 138.

upon it. It was only by chance, the article said, that any passengers could go east that winter, and when they were finally successful it was only after waiting several days for seats.

During the period of the gold rush to Idaho and Montana territories in 1864, passengers were constantly waiting in Atchison for seats in the westbound coaches. At this time the fare was four hundred fifty dollars, and in the mining regions the coaches carried a full load in each direction. In one day the Holladay Express office at Denver shipped sixty-eight thousand dollars in gold eastward on the Platte valley route.[121]

The Indian wars of 1864 and 1865 and the severe winter at the time of this trouble, delayed travel over the plains for a few months. However, in october 1864 passenger traffic and the mail business were so heavy that the Overland line refused to carry express freight weighing over five pounds. During the summer of 1866 one stage carried thirteen passengers to Denver at a fare of one hundred seventy-five dollars each.[122]

Holladay was a good advertiser. He attracted business through the leading newspapers of the west. An advertisement from the Laramie stage office was distributed over parts of four magazine pages. It gave detailed information to the traveling public, describing the new and comfortable Concord spring wagons

[121] Atchison (Kans.) *daily globe,* july 16, 1894; *Rocky mountain news* (Denver), october 19, 1866; Black Hawk (Colo. terr.) *mining journal,* january 16, 1864.

[122] *Ibid.,* december 12, 1864, january 13, 1865; *Rocky mountain news* (Denver), october 6, 1864, july 25, 1866.

and coaches, the meals at an average price of sixty
cents, location of telegraph offices along the line,
rates on transportation of treasure, freight, and express, stop-over privileges, and other information.
Passengers were allowed these privileges only if they
registered with the stage agent where they were stopping. A through ticket from Atchison to Placerville,
the advertisement said, could be bought for two hundred dollars, and the passenger was allowed twenty-
five pounds of baggage free.[123]

During the spring and summer of 1865 the Overland line was hauling what was considered to be a
large number of passengers. There were, in all,
eighty-three passengers from the west to Atchison,
which is not a large number according to present-day
standards, but which at that time indicated that the
Civil war was over and Indian depredations were
lessening. Before august 11 of that year passengers
paid one hundred seventy-five dollars each from Denver to Atchison. The following table gives the number of passengers and coaches arriving at Atchison
between may and september:

Month	Passengers	Coaches
May	12	3
June	18	6
July	20	7
August	15	4
September	18	3
Total	83	23

[123] Trails clippings (Library of Kansas state historical society), II,
no. II, 10.

ADVERTISEMENT FOR THE OVERLAND STAGE LINE, 1864

One coach in june delivered sixty-four sacks of mail in the eastern city.[124]

Although, unfortunately, there is no complete record of receipts on the Holladay stage lines, the annual report of Postmaster-general William Dennison in 1865 gives the receipts of two Holladay lines, although the amounts are grouped with those of two other stage routes.

ROUTE	PAY	RECEIPTS	EXCESS OF PAY
Salt Lake City to			
Folsom, Cal.	$385,000.00	$23,934.44	$726,065.56
Atchison to Salt			
Lake City	$365,000.00		
The Dalles to			
Salt Lake City	$186,000.00	$5,660.77	$180,339.23

According to the postmaster-general's report, he was disappointed with service on the eastern division of the main line because of its irregular schedule and low receipts. The Overland line's excuse had been that high water, bad roads, and hostile Indians had delayed the stagecoaches.[125]

From the beginning of his organization in 1862, Holladay had operated under most discouraging conditions, but, like the stagecoach king that he was, he carried on to the best of his ability and was undaunted by criticism. The main line was only one of his responsibilities. There was a growing number of branch lines to be supervised, and these were presenting a variety of problems to be solved.

[124] Atchison (Kans.) *daily free press*, may 8 to september 30, 1865.

[125] Postmaster-general's *report*, 1865, in U.S. House. *Executive documents*, 39 cong., 1 sess., VI, no. 1, 3, 14.

Branch Lines

Branch Lines

One of Holladay's unyielding ambitions had been to extend his stage lines as far as possible. When in 1862 the opportunity came to carry mail between Denver and near-by mining towns, he began at once to increase his stage routes. His first branch line was to Central City in Colorado territory. Located about halfway between Gregory Diggings and the upper mines in Nevada Gulch, Central City was an important mining center during the winter of 1861-1862. It had been founded in 1860 by Nathaniel Albertson, John Armour, and Harrison G. Otis. Empire City and Missouri City were mining towns near Central City, with Golden Gate two miles above and Black Hawk near-by. Several of the towns were joined together in one long canyon, but each retained its separate limits and government.[126]

Holladay's mail contract was to carry United States mail between Denver City and Missouri City for a period from july 1, 1862, to december 31, 1862, at the rate of $1870 yearly, and required sixteen-hour service on the forty-mile route. Post-offices along the route were Denver City, Arapahoe, Golden City, Mountain City, and Missouri City. Holladay received $935 by the preceding contract, and later car-

---

[126] Stone, *History of Colorado*, I, 150; U.S. Senate. *Executive documents*, 46 cong., 2 sess., V, no. 211, 11.

ried the United States mail on the same route under a new contract which paid $1842 a year and extended from january 1, 1863, to june 30, 1866. D. M. Barney and A. H. Barney acted as sureties for the contract, which required Holladay to exercise precautions in safeguarding the mail similar to those asked on the central route. He was obliged to give preference to transportation of United States mails and to deliver all mail assigned to the route or pay a financial forfeit for failure to do so. No fine could be more than three times the pay for the trip. Coach service was to be maintained tri-weekly in each direction on a sixteen-hour schedule. For this contract Holladay received $6447.

In december 1863 there was a demand for daily mail service on the branch line. An editorial appeared in a Black Hawk newspaper, saying,

Can't the people of the mines do something to procure a daily mail from Denver? We don't give a cent whether it is Ben Holladay or the department that is "approached" on the subject. Why should the privilege be extended to Denver and no farther?

The query brought forth no results that year. The schedule remained tri-weekly until february 17, 1864.[127]

Although the remuneration was small the mail contract on the Denver–Central City line was valu-

---

[127] *Ibid.,* 1, 15; Black Hawk (Colo. terr.) *mining journal,* november 30, december 21, 1863, february 16, 1864. Denver was often called Denver City in that time. The schedule was:

Leave Denver City, tuesday, thursday, saturday at 8 a.m.
Arrive Missouri City by 12 o'clock, night.
Leave Missouri City, monday, wednesday, friday at 8 a.m.
Arrive Denver City by 12 o'clock, night.

able because of passenger receipts in the thickly popu-
lated mining region. In august 1864 a passenger was
paying six dollars to ride from Central City to Denver City, but two days after this schedule of rates had
been advertised the fare was cut to five dollars from
Denver City to Central City, and to four from Central City to Denver. A competing line, giving daily
service between the two cities at half the rate charged
by the Overland, had forced the reduction in prices.
In december the fare was again raised. Round trip
between Denver City and Central City, including
dinners at one dollar and fifty cents each, went up to
twenty-five dollars. Service on sunday was suspended
january 1865.[128]

In january of the next year, the rival Butterfield
Overland Despatch line became a menace to the Holladay line on the Central City route. Holladay ruthlessly cut the passenger rate from ten dollars to one
dollar for the trip from Denver to Central City. The
Butterfield line, charging six dollars for the trip, was
injured by the cut, but continued the opposition
throughout the spring.

Holladay coaches from Central City did not make
close connections with the stages on the main line.
Passengers arriving from Central City at midnight
left Denver at eight in the morning to go west and
had to wait until three in the afternoon to go east.
However, there were advantages in the wait and little
complaint was made. The schedule was only slightly
improved in 1866 when the starting-time of the

[128] *Rocky mountain news* (Denver), august 2, 3, 5, 1864; Black Hawk
(Colo. terr.) *mining journal,* december 8, 1864, january 23, 1865.

coaches on the branch route was advanced from eight to seven o'clock in the morning.

The Central City line had the great advantage over the others of not being troubled by hostile Indians. It was, however, hindered in its operation for a few months of the year by bad roads and cold weather. During the fall and winter of 1863 there was more difficulty than usual. Deep snows made it necessary to replace the wheels of the coaches with runners, and the "sleighs" could not keep up the speed of the wheeled coach. During the following winter a coach upset at Clear creek. An inexperienced driver let the rear wheels drop into a deep rut covered with snow. The coach was hurled fifteen feet into a gulch, and the driver and one passenger were badly injured. In may 1864 it took two days for coaches to go between Denver and Black Hawk. On may 28 both westbound and eastbound coaches were halted on their trips. During a violent storm some of the horses had become exhausted and some had died. The next mail, two days later, was carried by buggy. Fresh livestock was sent from Denver and daily service was resumed the following week.[129]

A daily express stage ran between Denver and Black Hawk in 1863, leaving Black Hawk at seven-thirty in the morning and arriving at Denver at ten in the evening. Large quantities of express and treasure were hauled on the branch line. Some of the buyers shipped three hundred ounces of gold at a time,

129 *Ibid.*, november 30, 1863; *Rocky mountain news* (Denver), november 30, december 29, 1863, may 28, june 4, december 7, 1864; Atchison (Kans.) *daily free press*, february 6, 1866.

while Clark and company, bankers, shipped four hundred and thirty-four ounces of clear retort.[130]

In 1866 the mining industry began to decline. After selling much inflated stock in the east the companies quit working the mines. The reduction of gold ore was expensive and there was no demand for copper, silver, and lead. The inhabitants of the mining region near Denver moved away. By 1867 in the valley through Central City, Mountain City, and Black Hawk, abandoned mills could be seen for miles. Missouri City, on the hill westward from Central City, was almost a "ghost town," with its empty houses and mills and its silent flumes. Holladay, as usual, had profited at the right time; after his gains during the boom period he sold his stagecoach business before the depression was felt.[131]

In Nebraska territory the stagecoach business was less subject to fluctuations. Here Holladay became interested in two branch lines connecting with his main line at Fort Kearny. Although he did not have full control of these lines until after they had been operated for several years, they were important ones in his stagecoach system.

The branch line between Nebraska City, a center of freighting activity, and Fort Kearny was owned by the Western Stage company. In may 1862 D. L. Lushlough wrote to John H. Maxon that he had, two weeks previously, obtained the contract to carry the mail from Nebraska City to Kearney City once a

---

[130] Central City (Colo. terr.) *daily miner's register,* march 14, 1866; Black Hawk (Colo. terr.) *mining journal,* november 30, 1863.

[131] Smiley, *History of Denver,* 395, 399, 400.

week for four years. On may 10 the Honorable S. G.
Daily, Nebraska territorial delegate in congress, was
able to get the service increased to three weekly deliveries, and on may 31 it was announced that the
Western Stage company would begin tri-weekly service on july 1. The new route did not require ferries
or fords, and no delay was expected in the transportation of freight, express, or passengers. The distance
between the two cities was one hundred sixty-seven
miles, the route going by way of Syracuse, Palmyra,
and Olatha. The Western Stage company started mail
service on august 2, but did not put coaches on the
route until later. After these had been installed, passengers from Nebraska City often complained that
they were unable to get seats in the Holladay coaches
at Fort Kearny. In the fall of 1864 the company sold
its property to Holladay, who then established daily
service. After this it was possible for passengers from
Nebraska City to buy through tickets at that station
for points in Colorado, Idaho, and Montana territories, Utah and Nevada territories, and California.[132]

On march 27, 1865, Holladay secured a contract to
carry mail between Nebraska City and Kearney City
for seven thousand dollars a year. Service was to be

---

[132] Nebraska City *news,* may 11, 24, 31, august 2, 26, 1862; Morton,
History of Nebraska, I, 96. The stage line advertisement was:

Overland Stage Line

From Nebraska City, N.T.

To all principal points in Colorado, Utah,

Nevada, Idaho, Montana, California, and Oregon

Coaches leave Nebraska City daily

Through tickets for sale at the office

E. S. Hawley, Agent

Nebraska City

Ben Holladay, Proprietor

tri-weekly from january 1, 1865, to june 30 of the
next year. Holladay was to carry all mail, regardless of its size or weight, and to maintain a schedule
of five days twelve hours for the trip each way. Stations on the route were Nebraska City, Nursery Hill,
Palmyra, Saltillo, Camden, Arcola, and Kearney
City.[133] A good service was maintained in 1865. In
january of that year stagecoaches came from Denver
to Nebraska City in four and one-half days. This was
the record for all routes between Denver and the
Missouri river. Nebraska City proudly advertised:
"Through to the Rocky mountains from Nebraska
City by Ben Holladay's Overland coaches in four
days and a half."

The tri-weekly schedule was as follows:

Leave Nebraska City monday, wednesday, and friday at 6 a.m.
Arrive at Kearney City, fifth day by 6 p.m.
Leave Kearney City monday, wednesday, and friday at 6 a.m.
Arrive at Nebraska City, fifth day by 6 p.m.[134]

Nebraska City was not satisfied with this schedule,
however, and wanted a daily mail service westward.
In february 1866 the city announced that the daily
service would commence on or after the first day of
july. Consequently it was a severe blow when P. D.
Elking, Holladay agent, received a telegram on september 30 authorizing him to discontinue the mails
from Nebraska City to Fort Kearny. The new service
called for transportation of the Nebraska City mail
once a week by horseback or buckboard to Big Blue
on the main line. Holladay's contract to carry the

133 U. S. Senate. *Executive documents,* 46 cong., 2 sess., V, no. 211, 11, 12.
134 Nebraska City *news,* january 10, 1865.

mail on the Nebraska City–Fort Kearny route had paid him ten thousand five hundred dollars.[135]

His competitors, the Western Stage company, also operated the line from Omaha to Fort Kearny. In 1864 they were complaining that their passengers arriving at Fort Kearny from the northeast were denied seats in the coaches on Holladay's main lines. On october 30 of that year Holladay telegraphed from Salt Lake City to E. F. Hooker, superintendent of the Western Stage company:

You will continue to sell through tickets to Denver, at one hundred and fifty dollars. I will not discriminate against your passengers.

BEN HOLLADAY

Nevertheless, disputes continued in 1865, and in march Holladay bought the Western Stage company, thus effectively settling them. The sale gave him a profitable stage connection between Omaha and Fort Kearny, where he met the main line. The former company had operated a tri-weekly line and had suffered delays in transportation. Omaha was well pleased to hear the news. Under the Holladay management it expected a direct daily line of stages to be installed between that city and Denver and better service on the one hundred sixty-three mile run between Omaha and Fort Kearny.

The new business proved profitable for Holladay. His previous experience with branch lines contributed to the success of the Omaha route. After he took control in may, coaches left Omaha regularly for the west and were filled to capacity, despite the high fare of one hundred and fifty dollars. Service continued to

135 U.S. Senate. *Executive documents*, 46 cong., 2 sess., V, no. 211, I, 11, 12; Nebraska City *news*, february 6, october 6, 1866.

be tri-weekly. Coaches left Omaha every monday, wednesday, and friday at eight in the evening. A treasure and freight express in charge of a capable messenger was sent weekly from Omaha to Denver. The headquarters of the line, of which George M. Lloyd was agent, was an office below the Herndon House.[136]

In september 1865 Holladay secured a mail contract on the new line, which increased the service and also brought him $14,968 a year. The contract called for the transportation of the mails from Council Bluffs, Iowa, by way of Omaha and Grand Island City, to Fort Kearny and return, six times a week. The company was also required to make three weekly trips between Columbus and Genoa. Holladay was to be paid quarterly for the service between july 1, 1865, and june 30, 1866. John E. Russell and George Otis acted as sureties for the contractor. The main offices on the route were Council Bluffs, Omaha, Fremont, El Dorado, Columbus, Grand Island City, White Cloud, Fort Kearny, and Kearney City. A schedule of forty-eight hours was established between Council Bluffs and Kearney City and of four hours between Columbus and Genoa.[137]

---

136 *Ibid.*, august 26, 1865; Omaha *Nebraskian,* november 4, 1864, march 30, 1865; Omaha *weekly herald,* october 27, november 3, 10, 1865; Omaha *daily herald,* october 20, december 22, 1865.

137 U.S. Senate. *Executive documents,* 46 cong., 2 sess., v, no. 211, 1, 13, 14. No sunday service was given between Kearney City and Council Bluffs; the schedule was:

Leave Council Bluffs daily except sunday at 6 a.m.
Arrive Kearney City on third day by 6 a.m. – 48 hours.
Leave Kearney City daily except sunday at 6 a.m.
Arrive Council Bluffs on third day by 6 a.m. – 48 hours.
Leave Genoa tuesday, thursday, saturday at 1 p.m.
Arrive Columbus by 5 p.m.

The distances from Omaha by this route were as follows:

Omaha to Fort Kearny	193 miles
Omaha to Julesburg, Colorado	302 miles
Omaha to Fort Bridger, Wyoming	900 miles
Omaha to Salt Lake City, Utah	1060 miles
Omaha to Virginia City, Montana	1549 miles
Omaha to Boise City, Idaho	1860 miles

The stations on the Omaha–Fort Kearny division were from eight to twenty-three miles apart, but only two of thirteen stations were less than eleven miles from another stopping-place. Fremont, Columbus, and Grand Island were the principal way stations. Additional post-offices on the line were Elkhorn, Wallace, Buchanan, Brewer's ranch, Albeville, and Nebraska Center.[138]

During the fall of 1865 the Holladay line had what was considered a profitable business. Three coaches during october brought nineteen passengers from Omaha and fifteen persons traveled by stage from Kearney City and from points farther west. In november one coach carried six passengers from Omaha and three went as far as Fort Kearny. The passenger fares were reduced in april 1866. The following table shows the reduction in fares and schedule from Omaha to four western cities:

	FARE	TIME
Omaha to Denver	$125	5 days
Omaha to Salt Lake City	$250	9½ days
Omaha to Boise City	$350	12½ days
Omaha to Virginia City	$350	13 days

138 Omaha *weekly republican*, may 18, 1866. The distances of the different stations from Omaha on the Omaha–Fort Kearny division are given in the appendix.

It was cheaper to buy a through ticket from Omaha to Salt Lake City than to buy passage from Omaha to Denver and then from Denver to Salt Lake City. In the preceding schedule of fares a ticket between Denver and Salt Lake City cost one hundred and fifty dollars.[139]

The Omaha line passed through larger settlements than the Nebraska City line and served as a valuable feeder in 1865 and 1866. The Union Pacific railroad, advancing from Omaha, was responsible for its continued shortening during the term of Holladay's management.

---

[139] Omaha *weekly herald,* october 27, november 3, 10, 1865, march 30, 1866. The arrivals and departures of passengers at Omaha were:

ARRIVALS AT OMAHA

From:	Denver	Russell's	Fremont	Columbus	Salt Lake City	Elkhorn	Kearney City and Fort Kearny
Oct. 20, 1865	1				3		1
Oct. 22	3			3			
Oct. 26	5 and messenger						2 and messenger
Nov. 6		1		1	3	2	1
Mar. 30, 1866				2	1		2

DEPARTURES FROM OMAHA

For:	Denver	Russell's	Fremont	Columbus	Salt Lake City	Elkhorn	Kearney City and Fort Kearny
Oct. 20, 1865	1			1			2 and messenger
Oct. 25	1			1			
Nov. 6			1	2			3
Mar. 29, 1866		1		2		1	

In anticipation of this advance, Holladay sought new fields to tap farther west. He began to look into the possibilities of stage lines in Montana and Idaho territories. In 1860 Captain E. D. Pierce had discovered gold in Idaho territory along the south fork of the Clearwater river. By 1861 valuable mines were being developed in that field. In june the Oro Fino and Salmon mines were being worked and Lewiston was a booming town. A rush of miners to the Boise basin began in the spring of 1863. That valley region was rich in very promising minerals, lumber, and water supply. The towns of Placerville, Centerville, and Bannock were in the territory, which grew so rapidly in population that by 1864 over sixteen thousand people were living in the basin. Bannock was the largest town. Boise City had sprung up on the Oregon trail, close to a military post. The basin country apparently had suffered no great setback by the discovery of gold in Owyhee county in may 1863, when three thousand people had hurried from there to the new region. A few months after the gold discovery silver and quartz were discovered also, and the towns of Boonville, Ruby City, and Silver City were founded.[140]

Montana territory was also a rich mining field in 1864. Gold had been discovered at Bannock in the southwestern part in 1862, and at Alder Gulch, about seventy miles east during the following year. The latter settlement was called Virginia City after

---

[140] Brosnan, *History of Idaho*, 91, 94, 95; Camp Douglas (Utah terr.) *daily union vedette,* february 15, 1865. Boise was then commonly known as Boise City.

1864.[141] The mining centers located in Montana territory in 1865 had a population of eighteen thousand
two hundred, exclusive of people in Bitter Root valley and Hell-Gate Ronde. Alder Gulch, with its rich
ore, attracted many miners. In a week's time one company made eighteen hundred seventy dollars with the
aid of fourteen workers, and another made six hundred dollars in one week with three workers. In 1864
a miner named John Cowan, discovering rich gold
deposits in Last Chance gulch, opened up the Helena
City mining district which rivaled Virginia City.
During the first year of mining the Helena district
shipped out approximately sixteen million dollars
in gold.

The development of the mines in Idaho and Montana territories had early brought a demand for transportation between the mines and Salt Lake City. In
1863 the Oliver and Conover company established a
stage route between Salt Lake City and Virginia City,
which was so successful that it encouraged Holladay
to start a rival line.[142] It was reported in Salt Lake
City in march 1864, that Holladay was planning to
start a stage route from that point to Virginia City.
He had, in fact, secured a mail contract for service
between these two cities. In anticipation of this, his
agent, Superintendent Spotswood, traveled to the
Missouri river in Kansas to bring back two hundred
and ninety mules, thirty stages, and ten lumber

141 Harlow, *Old waybills*, 280.
142 Hebard, *Pathbreakers*, 207; Saunders, *History of Bannock county,
Idaho*, 88; Brown, *Fort Hall*, 353; The Dalles (Oregon) *weekly mountaineer*, september 15, 1865, august 17, 1866.

wagons. They were brought westward over the old California trail, crossing the South Platte river at Julesburg on june 2, and reaching Salt Lake City on june 29. Two days later the company was ready to commence both express and passenger service on the new road.

The agreement called for tri-weekly service between Fort Hall, Idaho territory, and Virginia City, for a compensation of $13,271 a year, between july 1, 1864, and june 30, 1868. By this contract Holladay received $53,084 from the United States government. Mail stations on the line were Fort Hall, Ogden, Cache Valley, Snake River Ferry, Bannock City, and Virginia City. These stations furnished so much express and such a large number of passengers that Holladay soon drove Oliver and Conover out of competition, after lowering fares in september to twenty-five dollars. The following year Oliver and Conover started an express line between Virginia City, Ophir, and Blackfoot, and carried mail between Helena City and Virginia City.

Holladay also secured two mail contracts from the government for service between Salt Lake City and the northwest. The agreement was for his company to carry the mail by tri-weekly service between Salt Lake City and The Dalles, Oregon, from july 1, 1864, to september 30 of that year at a rate of one hundred fifty-six thousand dollars a year. An additional contract was given him for service between october 1, 1864 and june 30, 1866, at a rate of one hundred eighty-six thousand dollars a year. Senator Benjamin F. Harding of Oregon had been working in Washington, D.C., to secure mail service between Salt Lake City and Walla Walla, Washington territory. On april 29, 1864, a newspaper at The Dalles published a letter from Harding which said, in part:

The mail from Salt Lake City to Walla Walla is already secured. We have by dint of persevering boring succeeded in getting the postmaster-general to let the contract for a tri-weekly four-horse coach service at $156,000 per year. Time, ten days for eight months and fourteen days for the balance of the year.[143]

On march 21, 1864, Holladay sent an agent from Salt Lake City to locate the new road and to supervise the building of stations and the placing of livestock. The work was not completed according to expectations by july 1, and it was august 11 before the first stage reached Boise City.[144] A schedule of forty-eight hours was established for service between The Dalles and Walla Walla, and another for fourteen days eight hours between Walla Walla and Salt Lake City. The report of Postmaster-general D. M. Key read that the United States government paid Holladay thirty-nine thousand dollars on the first contract extending to september 30, 1864, and three hundred twenty-five thousand dollars on the second contract ending june 30 two years later. Holladay gave a cheap sub-contract to Thomas and company to carry mail from Boise City to The Dalles, and this contract was held until 1866. In that year, Haley and Greathouse,

---

143 *Ibid.*, April 29, 1864; Saunders, *op. cit.*, 88; Sacramento *daily union,* march 31, april 1, 1864; Root and Connelley, *Overland stage,* 580; U.S Senate. *Executive documents,* 46 cong., 2 sess., V, no. 211, 1, 4, 12, 13. Montana territory was organized later in 1864.

144 The Dalles (Oregon) *weekly mountaineer,* august 5, 1864; Sacramento *daily union,* march 31, april 1, 1864.

who purchased the equipment of Thomas and company, assumed the agreement.[145]

Oliver and company as well as Holladay used the road from Salt Lake City to Bear River Junction, which covered eighty-three miles. From the Junction the Oregon road led to the west, passed Malad and Boise City, crossed the Snake river by ferry, and then followed the old Oregon trail to the Columbia river. Holladay used six-horse stages to carry the mail between Fort Hall and Salt Lake City. The entire length of the route was about one thousand miles. The main stations on the route were Salt Lake City, Farmington, Ogden City, Boise City, La Grande, Walla Walla, and The Dalles. David Street was made paymaster and general manager of the line between Salt Lake City and Boise City. In 1864 the passenger fare was one hundred dollars in gold between Salt Lake City and Boise City, and two hundred forty dollars between Walla Walla and Salt Lake City. Each passenger was allowed transportation of twenty-five pounds of baggage free, as on the main line, but express cost one dollar fifty cents a pound.[146]

[145] U.S. Senate. *Executive documents,* 46 cong., 2 sess., V, no. 211, 1, 4, 6. The schedule was:
Leave The Dalles monday, wednesday, friday at 10 a.m.
Arrive Walla Walla wednesday, friday, sunday by 10 a.m.
Leave Walla Walla monday, wednesday, friday at 10 a.m.
Arrive The Dalles wednesday, friday, sunday by 10 a.m.
Leave Walla Walla monday, wednesday, friday at 10 a.m.
Arrive Salt Lake City, fourteenth day by 6 p.m.
Leave Salt Lake City monday, wednesday, friday at 10 a.m.
Arrive Walla Walla, fourteenth day by 6 p.m.
[146] *Idaho daily statesman* (Boise), october 21, 1923; Rusling, *Great west,* 214; Hafen, *Overland mail,* 280; U.S. Senate. *Executive documents,* 46 cong., 2 sess., V, no. 211, 1, 4. Additional stations were Centerville,

Holladay, finding the business on the Oregon line to be lucrative, made every effort to maintain regular service. However, during the winter of 1864-1865 severe storms handicapped transportation to such an extent that travel between Salt Lake City and Boise City was delayed for days. A newspaper report of the time said that the bad weather would have closed the route entirely had it not been for the determination and perseverance of the Holladay agents and drivers. One mail was carried on pack horses through snow fifteen and twenty feet deep over the Bannock mountains. The bad weather lasted until april 1865.[147]

Travel on the Washington territory line during Holladay's ownership was not as heavy as that on the Montana line. The latter, developed to Virginia City, was in 1865 one of the best managed of the stage routes. The four-horse coaches, drawn by good livestock, averaged one hundred sixty miles a day traveling the five hundred miles between Salt Lake City and Virginia City. The route led from Salt Lake City to Bear River Junction, and through the Cache valley to Franklin, then crossed the Snake river by way of the Eagle Rock ferry. At intervals along the way were the home stations. At some of these, keepers raised vegetables on near-by plots of ground to vary the menu of beef, bacon, saleratus biscuit, and chicory coffee, served two or three times a day to travelers.[148]

Kaysville, Brigham City in Utah territory, Auburn in Idaho territory, Wallulla and Umatilla in Oregon.

[147] Elliott, *History of Idaho territory*, 301.

[148] Rusling, *Great west*, 220; San Francisco *daily evening bulletin*, november 14, 1865; Omaha *weekly herald*, june 20, 1866; Pollinger, letter to Callaway, 1, 2, MS. (Files of Montana state historical society).

Post-offices on the route were located at Ogden, Fort Hall, Cache Valley, Snake River Ferry, Bannock City, and Virginia City. There was a tri-weekly schedule of four days ten hours between Fort Hall and Virginia City during eight months of the year, and a weekly schedule of five days ten hours during the other four months.[149] The branch line to Virginia City made connections with the Salt Lake City–Boise City line.

High revenues from the rich mining section tended to offset Holladay's losses on the main stage line. It was considered to be a very good year in 1864 when five hundred passengers were hauled from Boise City to East Bannock. In june 1865 Holladay put new Concord coaches on the line; each coach, drawn by six horses, cost fifteen hundred dollars and accommodated seventeen passengers when the two top seats were used. In september of the same year coaches were reported to be filled with passengers. The larger part of the gold bullion from the Montana mines went by stage through the Snake river region to Salt Lake City. The fare between Boise City and Virginia

---

149 U.S. Senate. *Executive documents,* 46 cong., 2 sess., v, no. 211, 1, 6. The schedule was:

8 months   Leave Fort Hall monday, wednesday, friday at 8 a.m.
            Arrive Virginia City on fourth day by 6 p.m.
            Leave Virginia City monday, wednesday, friday at 8 a.m.
            Arrive Fort Hall on fourth day by 6 p.m.

4 months   Leave Fort Hall monday at 8 a.m.
            Arrive Virginia City on fifth day by 6 p.m.
            Leave Virginia City monday at 8 a.m.
            Arrive Fort Hall on fifth day by 6 p.m.

The fare in april 1866 from Salt Lake City to Virginia City was $175 in currency.

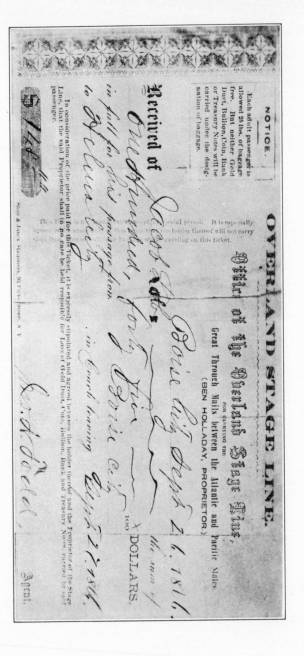

OVERLAND STAGE LINE TICKET, 1866

City was reduced that month from one hundred fifty to one hundred dollars, legal tender notes, and the stages covered the distance in three and one-half days. Coaches traveled from Salt Lake City to Virginia City in four days.[150]

The ticket used by Holladay on his Montana line stipulated that the holder, in consideration for the price paid, had agreed to waive responsibility of the proprietor for the loss of any bullion, gold dust, bank and treasury notes carried on the coach. This treasure was not classed as baggage under the free twenty-five pound clause.[151]

Holladay had no mail contract to Helena City, but he established a stage line between that point and Virginia City during the early part of june 1866. His former competitors, A. J. Oliver and company, already had a line between the two cities, and a third competitor, the California Stage company, under the direction of Al Guitwitz and Ben Stafford, was maintaining a six-horse daily stagecoach schedule on the route. The rivalry among the three companies was spirited, but ended with Holladay forcing the other two from the route by reducing his schedule from sixteen to ten hours for the one hundred and twenty-five mile trip and reducing fares to two dollars and fifty cents. No sooner was the field clear than the low fare was raised to "$25.00 in clean gr. bankable gold

---

150 Camp Douglas (Utah terr.) *daily union vedette,* september 7, 12, 21, 26, 1865; Saunders, *History of Bannock county, Idaho,* 90, 91; Atchison (Kans.) *daily free press,* may 17, 1865; *Idaho daily statesman* (Boise), october 21, 1923.

151 See Munson, "Pioneer life in American history" in *Journal of American history,* I, 103.

dust or $37.50 in green backs or 'Lincoln' skins as they were called."

In september 1866 a quantity of express was shipped from Montana territory, and many passengers journeyed from Virginia City. The following fares were being paid:

> Virginia City to Boise City..............................$125
> Boise City to Sale Lake City..........................$100
> Boise City to Missouri river..........................$400
> ($100 gold and $300 legal tender)[152]

The Montana territory line had connections at Virginia City for towns in northern Idaho territory, Oregon, and the Columbia river. Travelers could also board coaches at Boise City for Salt Lake City on the main route and then change to Holladay stages going eastward to Denver and Atchison, or they could travel westward by coach from Salt Lake City to California. The fares were high, but the successful miners in the northern regions were well able to afford them, and the great expense of operating the lines seems to have justified the cost of travel.[153]

Holladay's lucrative branch lines helped to bring civilization to the remote sections of the west, and through the United States mail service to keep the settlers in these sections in closer touch with the east

---

[152] Atchison (Kans.) *daily free press,* september 6, 1865; *Rocky mountain news* (Denver), august 2, 1866; The Dalles (Oregon) *weekly mountaineer,* september 28, 1866; Pollinger, letter to Callaway, 1, 2, MS. (Files of Montana state historical society).

[153] Sacramento *daily union,* september 15, 1866; Camp Douglas (Utah terr.) *daily union vedette,* february 10, 1866; *Montana democrat* (Virginia City), april 12, 1866.

at a time when the unity of the nation was threatened. The mining industry would have suffered greatly without the efficient service provided by Holladay. That he was able to provide this service while taxed to the utmost with a variety of problems and difficulties is further proof of his native ability and shrewdness.

Difficulties with Weather, Highwaymen,
and Indians

Difficulties with Weather, Highwaymen, and Indians

During the years from 1862 to 1866 Holladay encountered more than his share of trouble. He was operating between three and four thousand miles of stagecoach lines, running through widely different regions and presenting every kind of problem. The one most difficult to solve was that of the weather. The general attitude of the public was that the stagecoach must come through regardless of conditions. Consequently the drivers were forced to make their runs during severe storms, under great danger from exposure, loss of direction, and accident.

The most severe snow-storm in twenty years was reported during january 1865. The coach, driven by Ab Williamson, left Middle Boulder, Colorado territory, about four o'clock one january afternoon. An army officer from Fort Laramie, an Atchison merchant with his eighteen-year-old daughter, two miners, and a Holladay mule buyer were passengers. An express messenger was in charge of the coach. After they left Middle Boulder the weather seemed to be growing worse. The heavy fall of snow made footing precarious and vision difficult. Williamson urged his team along until it was stopped by a deep drift, from which men and horses together were unable to pull the coach. The passengers prepared for a bitter siege. Their only food was the stage-driver's lunch and some sandwiches brought by the girl, but the driver cheered the passengers with a bottle of good wine and rationed out the food and drink. Meanwhile the army officer and the miners volunteered to go for aid. Reaching St. Vrain they told the news of the snow-bound stage and a volunteer group started at once to the rescue. In a few hours they had dug out the coach and freed the passengers, who had been prisoners of the storm for two days and nights. No serious results were suffered.

Rain was as much an enemy as snow. Extremely heavy downpours often caused washouts on the road and stagecoaches were delayed until raging streams subsided sufficiently for the driver to ford them. However, as the stagecoach was still the best means of travel in the west, passengers were willing to risk their safety and soon learned to expect wet clothing and long delays.

Less calmly they anticipated a possible hold-up by road agents. Beyond any curve in the road one or more highwaymen might be waiting, masked and with ominously leveled muskets. Under threat of instant death they would rob the messenger of his treasure box and the passengers of their valuables. Usually they let their victims go unharmed bodily but very "empty in pocket and sheepish in feelings."

In the end these outlaws were usually executed. Vigilantes, substituting for the law, were swift in bringing judgment. Jack Slade is a famous example. He had been an efficient division agent for Ben Holladay until drunkenness caused his discharge. He then went to Virginia City and turned ruffian. There he was fined for threatening a judge who displeased him. Vigilantes warned him to leave the region, but he stayed until the citizens hanged him.[154]

Robbers had regular headquarters along the Idaho and Montana stage lines and, like the more honorable secret societies, had regular initiation services and mystic signs. They planned to rob coaches and passengers who carried money on those stage routes. On november 8, 1864, an overland stage was stopped near Idaho City by three masked road agents with shotguns. They compelled the three passengers to leave the coach, searched them and took one thousand four hundred forty dollars.

Robbers were not always highwaymen. One robbery which occurred in november 1864 was attributed to a passenger. Although a messenger accompanied the coach he was apparently off-guard when someone unbuckled one strap on the boot of the stage and stole a sack of mail. The trip to Atchison was made without discovery of the theft, but a few days later Ray Grayson, agent at a station near Whisky Run, a small stream one hundred fifty miles west of Atchison, discovered the mail-bag on the prairie. Letters and papers were scattered on the ground. The coach messenger, Frank Root, came to the scene of the robbery from Atchison, collected and forwarded all mail with legible addresses, and sent the rest to the dead letter office. Communication between Samuel O.

---

[154] Clemens, *Roughing it,* 94-97; Richardson, *Beyond the Mississippi,* 497.

Jerome, division agent at Big Sandy station in Nebraska territory, and W. A. Gillespie, agent at Atchison, uncovered the fact that the robber was a passenger named G. G. Wheeler, who had bought a stage ticket from Rock Creek, Dakota territory to Atchison. Although special agents were put on his trail by the United States postal department, no record has been found that Wheeler was captured. This was the only loss of mail the stage messenger suffered, although he handled over ten thousand sacks of mail between 1863 and 1867.

On july 13, 1865, a southbound stage from Montana territory was attacked. The stage was stopped in Portneuf canyon in Idaho territory, at a spot which was then a haven for the outlaws menacing the route between Butte and Salt Lake City. It was later believed that Frank Williams, driver of the stage, had betrayed his passengers to the gang led by Jim Locket. When the coach reached the appointed place a cry came from the woods, "Boys, here they are." Several volleys were fired into the coach, and the passengers answered with buckshot. Four of the passengers were killed and two seriously wounded. The robbers took seventy thousand dollars in gold and other valuables, then escaped through the bushes. In about ten days Williams resigned and went to Salt Lake City, where he spent money freely, then traveled on to Denver to spend more. The vigilantes finally caught and hanged him to a tree on Cherry creek.[155]

---

[155] Atchison (Kans.) *daily free press,* july 13, 18, 1865; San Francisco *daily evening bulletin,* december 2, 1864; Clampitt, *Echoes from the Rocky mountains,* 81; Root and Connelley, *Overland stage,* 563, 564.

In 1865 one of the Holladay stages was held up by
five outlaws near Bitter creek, Idaho territory. The
messenger, at the time of the hold-up, was guarding
the treasure, which was under the driver's seat. It was
in a box made of strong sole leather and was iron-
bound and chained to the coach. There was only one
passenger besides the division blacksmith, who was
journeying to a way station. The highwayman dashed
out from the sagebrush and covered the victims, then
jerked the treasure box loose and took it into the
brush. The driver went at top speed to the nearest
station, telegraphed Bob Spotswood, superintendent
of the line, who was then at Fort Steele. A posse was
organized by Spotswood and Steele, another Holladay superintendent, to trail the robbers. The chase
was finally given up when the trail was lost in lava
rock country. But in 1867 one of the robbers con-
fessed. "Broncho Jack," a noted outlaw from California, had committed crimes in that state and was
returned from Texas for trial. At the trial he admitted his part in the Bitter creek robbery and impli-
cated other men. Only one man was caught. He was
killed in a stagecoach by a deputy sheriff after the
outlaw had refused to surrender. "Broncho Jack" was
given a life sentence.

Holladay himself experienced a hold-up. He was
traveling with his wife on the main line between
Denver and Salt Lake City when the stage was
stopped by two robbers. One of them covered the
driver, while the other thrust a big shotgun into the
coach. Holladay had no time to draw a gun. He was
anxious that his wife, who was ill at the time, and

sleeping, should not be wakened. "Throw up your hands and don't stir!" the outlaw threatened. "Give us your money." Holladay was carrying about forty thousand dollars in a money-belt, an expensive watch and chain, an eight thousand dollar emerald pin, and several hundred dollars in his pocket. When told to "shell out quick" he did a little bluffing himself. He handed over the loose money in his pocket along with the watch and chain which weighed about five pounds, saying hurriedly, "There, there's every cent I've got. Take it and let me go. My wife is very ill, and I don't know what would happen to her if she knew what was going on."

The road agent was in no hurry to go. He told Holladay to keep his hands up and to stay quiet. Searching the stage for a treasure box the robbers found that none was being carried. About this time the hairs of Holladay's long mustache began to tickle his nose. He wanted very much to scratch, and told his guard as much, but the fellow, lacking sympathy, answered, "I'll blow a hole through you if you move your hands to do it." Holladay stood the torture as long as he could, then repeated his request. Then the road agent, apparently relenting, said, "Well, keep your hands still and I'll scratch it for you." He pushed the barrel of his gun quickly toward Holladay's face and dragged it over his nose, taking off so much skin that the victim was quite ready to assure the agent that the nose itch was entirely gone. Within a few minutes both men left. Holladay was thankful that he had been able to save his money-belt with its treasure and his valuable emerald. The de luxe private coach rolled on its way, while he rubbed his nose and his wife continued sleeping.[156]

Despite such hazards Holladay was compelled to travel over his lines several times a year for the purpose of inspection and consultation with his officials. One of his greatest concerns was the supply of feed for his livestock, which during the time of Indian wars was constantly threatened. Holladay's feed bill was estimated to average about one million dollars a year. Two thousand animals were fed daily. Approximately twenty thousand tons of hay a year were used which cost him about five hundred thousand dollars.

In 1866 sufficient feed to maintain the livestock in good condition was kept at about one hundred and fifty stations. Each station used from forty to eighty tons of hay a year. At normal times one hundred tons were kept at each station, but during the times of Indian war the amount was cut to fifty tons. Some of the stations owned hayfields near-by; others had the hay hauled from seventy-five to one hundred miles. When there was trouble from the Indians it was necessary to send out armed guards with the hay-cutters. The cost of hay necessarily varied according to the distance it had to be transported and the danger from Indian attack. The prices ran from fifteen to forty dollars a ton, and in 1865 reached a height of fifty dollars. Grain was fed to the animals, and this supply, also, was subject to variation.

In order to keep fresh relays for the incoming coaches and to replace crippled and sick livestock, the stage company kept from eight to twelve horses or

[156] Root and Connelley, *Overland stage,* 559.

mules at each station. Oats, barley, and corn were
their principal feed. An average of twelve quarts of
grain was fed daily to each animal, making the total
amount of daily feed for the two thousand head of
livestock about seven hundred fifty bushels.[157] In
peace times corn for the eastern division of the stage
line was bought in Nebraska territory and Kansas for
seventy-five cents to one dollar a bushel, plus the
transportation cost of nine or ten cents a pound. The
grain was delivered, usually, in sacks holding two
bushels and one peck each. In 1862 two trains with
grain for Holladay stations were stalled by snow at
Cheyenne pass in the Black hills. The contractor was
forced to buy another trainload of feed at Denver
which cost twenty cents a pound delivered to Fort
Halleck and North Platte stations. Although the original cost of the grain was only fifteen cents, freighters charged five cents a pound for transportation.

In 1864 the stage line was able to buy grain at Fort
Kearny for six cents a pound, but at Julesburg the
same year, after a serious Indian raid, it cost twenty
cents a pound. When Brigadier-general P. E. Connor,
making plans for an Indian campaign, offered ten
dollars a bushel at Fort Kearny for grain to be delivered at Julesburg, the offer was accepted by Henry
Carlyle, manager of a freighting firm which hauled
feed and wood for Holladay. Carlyle was unable to
deliver the ten thousand bushels contracted for and
had to wait from may 1 to june 14 before he could
find teamsters willing to risk the dangers of the trip.

---

[157] *Ibid.,* 74; *McClure's magazine,* XXVI, 87; U.S. Senate. *Miscellaneous
documents,* 46 cong., 2 sess., I, no. 19, 36, 37.

Teamsters who usually charged from twenty to twenty-five dollars a month charged from fifty to seventy-five dollars at such times. On another occasion Holladay ordered Carlyle to take a trainload of grain from Nebraska City to Julesburg. Indians had destroyed the supply at Julesburg, and Holladay was anxious to put his line in operation as soon as possible. Carlyle loaded each six-mule wagon with sixty-five sacks of oats and started west for Julesburg. Because of a drouth, as well as destruction by the Indians, there was no grass for the livestock, and they had to be fed grain, with the result that from the supply of sixty-five sacks to each wagon fifty-five each were consumed by the mules which did the hauling.

Holladay endeavored to have two hundred and fifty sacks of grain at each station. Oats were about five dollars a sack, and one-hundred-pound sacks of barley cost fifteen dollars. So great was the cost of grain, due in part to Indian depredations, that Holladay was believed to have spent at least six hundred thousand dollars a year for that item alone.[158]

The resentment of the Indians against the white man, which had been smouldering for a long time, broke into active rebellion in 1862. The emigrants, they said, had invaded their lands and endangered their good hunting grounds. The United States government was accused of bad faith in breaking the Indian treaties and failing to make gifts. The rebellion

[158] *Ibid.;* U.S. Senate. *Report,* 46 cong., 2 sess., I, no. 216, 12, 13. A writer in *McClure's magazine* (XXVI, 87, 88) wrote that Superintendent Dave Street went to St. Louis in 1864 and bought enough corn for Holladay livestock to fill seven Missouri steamers.

was timely. With the Civil war going on in the south
and east, and western troops being constantly withdrawn, the Indians had been urged by renegade
whites to attack the property of the Overland Stage
line between Fort Bridger and Salt Lake City. Some
of the Mormons were southern sympathizers, and
they were also suspected as the cause of some uprisings. The Snakes and the Bannocks led in the depredations on the Holladay property. These attacks resulted in the following losses to Holladay:

192 horses and mules
4 oxen and one cow
153 sacks of barley
220 sacks of corn
3 tons of hay
71 sets of harness damaged or destroyed
480 empty sacks damaged or destroyed
2 stagecoaches damaged or destroyed

In addition, several stations were damaged. The total
losses to Holladay in 1862, according to claims presented to congress later, amounted to $51,543.[159]

The depredations on the Holladay line during
march and april 1862 caused the postmaster-general
to issue an order suspending mail service on that
route. To insure delivery it was arranged that the mail
be carried by steamers to the east from San Francisco until further notice. This type of service was
continued until june 15 of that year, when the overland
transportation was resumed for the first-class mail.

[159] U.S. Senate. *Miscellaneous documents,* 46 cong., 2 sess., I, no. 19, 3-9,
54, 55; *Report,* 46 cong., 2 sess., I, no. 216, 12, 13. A detailed chart of
losses is given in the appendix.

brother, who was agent at Salt Lake City, to send mail or passengers eastward during the early part of may. He had called out mounted men to drive the Indians from the territory, but the stage service had not been resumed. On two hundred miles of the route across the plains livestock had been lost and there were only three hundred sixty soldiers under General Craig to protect four hundred miles of stage line. In may there were four companies of soldiers scattered along the line beyond Fort Laramie. Encouraged by the assistance he was now promised, Holladay went vigorously ahead with his plans for reopening the line. He reached Atchison from the east on may 10, and arrived in Denver on may 31, but by june 7 the daily mail service between St. Joseph and Salt Lake City had not yet been reopened.

The mail had been held up for so long that in the early part of june Julesburg had a warehouse packed full of it. As reported by a traveler at Carson City, who told of the mail blockade at Julesburg, nine mail-sacks and seven Wells, Fargo express-sacks had been burned at Sweetwater and twenty-one sacks of mail cut open at Ice Springs. The latter was the same theft reported by Colonel Burton and Senator Hooper, and with the traveler's report came the same expression of belief that the Indians had been led by renegade white men.[166]

In his trip from Denver to Salt Lake City, Holladay was able to see the extent of the damage to his

<hr>

[166] *Ibid.*, I, no. 19, 55; Sacramento *daily union,* may 9, june 7, 28, 1862; San Francisco *daily evening bulletin,* may 27, 1862; *Freedom's champion* (Atchison), may 10, 1862.

property on the South pass and Fort Laramie road. The region was the favorite hunting ground of the Snakes, Cheyennes, Arapahoes, and Sioux, who had expressed their disapproval of the stagecoach invasion with cruel effectiveness. The companies sent at General Craig's request were too few to protect the present route, and Holladay was considering a change from it, since it would always be dangerous as long as the Indians were able to fight for it. When the news had come to him in april of the raids on his property between Ham's Fork and Horseshoe creek, he had decided to give up his mail contract and to withdraw his property until protection could be secured.

Before making his trip west Holladay had conferences in Washington. He conferred with Postmaster-general Blair, and Secretary of War Stanton was asked to give protection to the line. Blair and Holladay, with Senator Milton Latham of California, made a call upon President Lincoln. The president was sympathetic. "Mr. Holladay," he said, "You must have protection; the mails must be carried." Holladay suggested that, since the military posts in the west were so scattered, President Lincoln ask Brigham Young to raise soldiers for the protection of the line. The president favored the idea and promised to push the matter. Holladay told him that the stage line could not be operated unless he could secure payment for his losses and protection in the future. Lincoln's reply was, "You may rest assured congress will fully reimburse you." Holladay then discussed with the postmaster-general the advisability of a new route south of the old South pass trail. Blair told him to use any route he wanted, but to get the mail to the Pacific.[167]

After this Holladay proceeded westward. At Fort Laramie he was joined by General Craig in an inspection of the route. They found all stations west of the fort destroyed, and mail scattered on the plains. All livestock between Fort Laramie and South pass was gone. At Salt Lake City Holladay decided definitely to move the stage line between Julesburg and Green River. The Bridger pass route, which he planned to use, lacked good water, grass, and wood, but there was less danger from Indians. He sent an agent to Fort Bridger to secure tents and stakes, teams, mechanics and supplies, and to locate and build stations on the new route. The order for removal was given july 8, 1862. Twenty-six stations, estimated to have cost twenty-five thousand dollars, were deserted, and a large supply of grain, valued by Superintendent Isaac Eaton at twenty-five thousand dollars, was abandoned. The supply station at Horseshoe creek included the blacksmith shop, coach shops, harness shops, warehouses, lodging houses, offices, and corrals, all of which were a complete loss.

At the time of the change Holladay was using one hundred and ten coaches, seventeen hundred and fifty horses and mules, and about four hundred and fifty men. His daily expense was heavy. Forage and supplies were hauled to the new stations, and ferries, bridges, and roads were built. Until permanent head-

---

[167] Sacramento *daily union,* june 28, 1862; U.S. Senate. *Miscellaneous documents,* 46 cong., 2 sess., I, no. 19, 51, 54, 55, 61.

quarters could be built by labor hired from Denver and Salt Lake City the employees lived in huts and tents.

The fact that the stage company did not break its regular schedule of mails in making a change of route is further evidence of Holladay's executive ability. On july 31, 1862, a Holladay employee, Major Kerr, arrived at Salt Lake City after a stage trip over the Cherokee trail, as the new road was called. It was so named because the Cherokees had come that way on their journey to California in 1849. Kerr reported that the new line was stocked and new stations were being built. The division agent, Jack Slade, had transferred all livestock, numbering three hundred and fifty horses and mules and some cattle, from Devil's Gate to Julesburg, and had placed all wagons and coaches of his division on the new line. Although Kerr found the old route preferable because of its superior water, he admitted that the new one was free from Indians, and he believed that a stage would be able to average ten miles an hour on the trip.

The Cherokee trail was many miles south of the former road. The nearest Indians were the Sioux, Crows, and Snakes, who were at least two hundred miles north, and the Utes one hundred miles south. Fort Halleck was built between North Platte and Rock Creek in august and furnished protection for the sixty-five miles of stage road between those stations until Fort Sanders was constructed in 1866. Holladay believed, nevertheless, that the United States government should send more troops westward to guard the mail line. On august 26, 1862, the day before he was to start for Washington, D.C., he telegraphed Postmaster-general Blair from Salt Lake City as follows:

Sir: A general war with nearly all tribes of Indians east of the Missouri river is close at hand. I am expecting daily an interruption on my line, and nothing but prompt, decisive action on the part of the government will prevent it.

He asked that more soldiers be placed along the line at points one hundred miles apart, declaring that the troops in the west were insufficient to protect the route and that Colonel Connor's forces, which were then on the march from California, were still four hundred miles westward.[168]

General Craig, in command of the troops protecting the overland mail routes, telegraphed Governor Harding of Utah territory that Secretary Stanton had authorized him to use Mormon volunteers again if necessary. Brigham Young was asked to furnish equipment for men and horses and all commissary supplies. General Craig himself favored the idea and believed that the Mormons would volunteer for service.[169] By october 26 Colonel Connor had established Camp Douglas near Salt Lake City. Besides the camp there were a post-office and a telegraph office. Connor commanded a headquarters company and five companies of the California volunteers, a total of three hundred eighty-two men.

---

[168] *Ibid.*, I, no. 19, 4, 11, 55, 60-66; Sacramento *daily union*, july 19, 1862; U.S. Department of interior, office of Indian affairs, commissioner's *report*, 1862, no. 43, 214; Coutant, *History of Wyoming*, I, 386.

[169] Sacramento *daily union*, september 3, 1862; Coutant, *op. cit.*, I, 381, 382. Two Nevada territory regiments were added to Connor's command.

The Indians in Dakota territory were showing new signs of enmity. In november one hundred head of horses belonging to traders and trappers were stolen near Fort Bridger. Colonel Connor began placing soldiers on the eastbound coaches for the protection of mail, express, and passengers. However, he was not pleased by the request for more soldiers to protect the stages. On december 20 he wrote the war department, suggesting that the reason Judge W. A. Carter, who was agent for the Overland Stage line and sutler of Fort Bridger, wanted to see more soldiers on the line, was that he sold supplies to the troops. He said also that Brigham Young wanted to have the four regiments of Camp Douglas soldiers scattered eastward along the stage route.

Colonel Connor had previously decided to garrison Fort Bridger and Ham's Fork, and on december 2, 1862, had sent Company I under Captain M. G. Lewis to Fort Bridger. As the Indians had recently attacked the Big Sandy telegraph station as well as the stage station at Pacific Springs, ten soldiers were left at the former place for the winter. After making the one hundred twenty mile march from Salt Lake City in five days, Captain Lewis had arrived at Fort Bridger on december 7. Seventy-four soldiers were in the company. On december 24 Colonel Connor sent a sergeant and seven privates as escorts for a provision train to Little Sandy. Detachments were also sent out from the fort during january and february of 1863 for escort and patrol duty along the line.[170]

[170] Coutant, *History of Wyoming*, I, 384; Post returns Fort Bridger, december 1862, january, february, 1863, MS. (War department, old records division, Washington, D.C.).

In january 1863 Colonel Connor decided to send out a military expedition against the Bannock and Snake Indians along the Bear river. Seventy-eight men of the Third California volunteers, under Captain C. H. Hoyt, left the post on january 22 for scout duty. Two hundred thirty-three men of the Second cavalry, California volunteers, under Colonel Connor and Majors Edward McGarry and M. F. Gallagher, left with two howitzers on january 24. Five days later the forces reached Bear river, one hundred fifty miles from Camp Douglas, and engaged in battle with the Indians. Three hundred of them were strongly entrenched in a blind ravine. Great courage was shown on both sides in the battle which lasted for four hours. Nineteen of Connor's men were killed outright, and thirty-eight, some of whom died of their wounds, were injured. The Indians lost two hundred twenty-four men in battle. One hundred seventy-five horses and a large quantity of arms were captured, while their lodges and provisions were destroyed under military order. Colonel Connor, returning with his troops to Camp Douglas on february 4, was promoted to the rank of Brigadier-general because of this successful campaign.[171]

The Snakes and Bannocks, fearing the soldiers at Camp Douglas, now ceased their depredations. The Utes, however, attacked a station at Sweetwater in april. They were driven off by soldiers of the Eighth (later the Eleventh) Ohio cavalry. General Connor believed that the Indians, urged on by Mormons,

[171] *Ibid.*, february 10, 1863; Sacramento *daily union*, february 17, april 11, 1863.

might now break up the Overland route and make the
emigrant road impassable. He telegraphed Major-
general H. W. Halleck at Washington for reinforce-
ments. General Halleck sent the message on to General John M. Schofield of the department of the
Missouri, who then ordered Colonel J. M. Chivington to send cavalry to the aid of General Connor.
Four companies of the First Colorado cavalry under
Major E. W. Wynkoop were sent to Fort Bridger,
but there was a delay in getting equipment, with the
result that Connor's forces had already defeated the
Utes in a battle west of Salt Lake City before the
Colorado cavalry had arrived.[172]

Nine companies of soldiers in Utah territory were
detailed by General Connor to guard the Holladay
line from Salt Lake City to Pacific Springs and also
the one from Fort Bridger to Bannock City. Captain
Lewis left Fort Bridger on june 9 to relieve Lieutenant W. T. Kittredge, who was leading soldiers in
an Indian scouting expedition. The party returned to
the post on june 21 with forty-nine Shoshones. Thirty-
six men of Company I, Third infantry, California
volunteers, were on detached service in june attempt-
ing to check Indian raids on the line, and other soldiers in the territory were used to escort emigrant
trains and to protect the stage company's property.

The military activities had their effect. In july between six and eight hundred Shoshones attended a
parley to make peace with General Connor and Gen-

[172] Coutant, *History of Wyoming*, I, 394, 396. Contemporary writers
often referred to brigadier-generals and major-generals by the simple
term of general, and the writer has followed this custom to some extent
to avoid repeated references to Brigadier-general Connor.

eral Doty of Utah territory. Blaming the Bannocks for leading them on the warpath, they returned one hundred and fifty stolen horses and mules. However, fifty warriors with their families had failed to surrender, and Connor was obliged to send one hundred and eight men, soldiers and officers, after them.

The Indian treaty lessened the necessity for soldiers, and the detachments on the mail line between Fort Bridger and Weber river were returned to the post in july. Company I, Third infantry, California volunteers, had been used largely to protect the overland route near Fort Bridger. However, a new duty was assigned to them in that month. Soldiers were sent to Ham's Fork to administer the oath of allegiance to the United States government. All persons entering Utah territory from the east, who had not previously taken the oath, were obliged to do so before entering the country of the Mormons.

During the summer of 1863 General Connor had soldiers stationed along the Overland line to protect the Holladay property and telegraph stations. Fort Bridger reported no engagements with the Indians in july. The southern Utes, under Little Soldier, made peace with General Connor in that month, with both Indians and soldiers exchanging captured property. Black Hawk, Ute Pete, and other Ute chiefs made a peace treaty near Springville, Utah territory about the same time.[173]

In the fall of 1863 log houses were built at Camp

[173] *Ibid.,* I, 398, 399; Post returns Fort Bridger, july 1863, MS. (War department, old records division, Washington, D.C.); Sacramento *daily union,* may 20, june 19, 1863; San Francisco *daily evening bulletin,* june 9, 1863.

Douglas to accommodate the California volunteers. Also stationed at the camp, in addition to six companies of the Third infantry and four of the Second cavalry, California volunteers, were two companies of Nevada cavalry and one of artillery. Fort Bridger had one company of infantry and one of cavalry under Major Gallagher. One company was stationed at Camp Connor and two were detailed at Camp Ruby, Idaho territory. There were about fifteen hundred men under General Connor in the four posts.[174]

The eastern end of the main line had also suffered from depredations in 1863. During the spring, troops along the stage route in Nebraska territory had been withdrawn for service in the Civil war. Acting-governor A. S. Paddock of Nebraska territory had protested the removal to no avail. Depredations were not numerous in that region, however, in 1863. During the summer thirty-four mules valued by R. L. Pease, Holladay employee, at sixty-eight hundred dollars were taken by Indians from the stage line near Fort Halleck and were never recovered.

In september a commission headed by George Evans was sent from Denver to make peace with the Cheyennes, Sioux, and Arapahoes. Its purpose was to extinguish the Indian claims to lands between the Platte river and the Rocky mountains. However, only a few chiefs attended the meeting and they could not be persuaded to sign the treaty.[175]

---

[174] *Ibid.*, november 20, 1863.

[175] Coutant, *History of Wyoming*, I, 395; Denver *weekly commonwealth*, september 24, 1863; U.S. Senate. *Miscellaneous documents*, 46 cong., 2 sess., I, no. 19, 3.

During the fall of 1863 the tribes in the region east of Denver appeared to have no hostile intentions. The white men along the overland trail were living in a false sense of security, which was to be rudely destroyed by the Indian war of 1864, and Holladay himself was to face the severest test of his entire career as a stagecoach manager.

More Indian Problems

More Indian Problems

At the outbreak of the Civil war the problem of military supervision in the west had been immediately recognized. California, Oregon, and the territories of Nevada and Colorado, with inhabitants of various nationalities, were at the time almost isolated from the rest of the United States. The west was organized into military districts and departments during the first few months of the war. The department of the West included territory from the Missouri river to the Rocky mountains, while the department of the Pacific included the rest of the country beyond the Rockies, with the exception of Utah territory. In november 1861 the department of Kansas was organized to supervise from Fort Leavenworth the regions of the territories of Nebraska, Dakota, Colorado, and Indian territory.

In 1864 the district of Nebraska, which embraced most of the territories of Nebraska, Dakota, and parts of Utah and Idaho, was under the command of General Robert B. Mitchell, brevet-major-general. Under orders from Fort Leavenworth and the United States war department, he was supposed to protect the overland mail route, but with only six hundred and eighty soldiers at his command to cover eleven hundred miles of road menaced by thousands of Sioux, Arapahoes, Cheyennes, Apaches, Comanches, and white outlaws, he could not provide much protection.[176]

Since 1862 the Indians had been accumulating the swift horses of the Holladay line; they were frequently better mounted and better armed than the soldiers, and their horses could outrun the government mounts. Often the outcome of the military encounters would depend upon whether or not the horses of the soldiers were too tired to pursue the enemy.

In the spring of 1864 depredations commenced along the South Platte. The overland route from Green River to Cottonwood was soon threatened. During the first part of april the Cheyennes, who had stolen livestock from the Bijou ranch, were dispersed at Fremont's Orchard by a part of the First cavalry under Lieutenant W. K. Dunn. The first real battle of the war occurred in may at Cedar Canyon, one hundred forty miles down the Platte river from Denver, when Major Jacob Downing led a company of the First Colorado cavalry to victory against the Cheyennes. Thirty-eight Indians were killed, and the village and several hundred ponies were captured.[177]

On may 23 Indians captured an Overland wagon near Cottonwood Springs, killed two men, fired the wagon, and captured the horses. As hostilities were reported from various points along the road, fear spread to the city of Denver. In june Governor John

---

176 U.S. Senate. *Miscellaneous documents,* 46 cong., 2 sess., I, no. 19, 59, 61.

177 *Ibid.,* I, no. 19, 19; Black Hawk (Colo. terr.) *mining journal,* april 14, 1864; *Rocky mountain news* (Denver), may 4, 1864; Smiley, *History of Denver,* 404.

Evans ordered all business houses closed at six-thirty every night, and all able-bodied men were drilled for defense. The killing of the Hungate family near Denver later in june caused the governor to place the city under martial law. Travel on the plains was checked, and foodstuffs became so scarce that the people in the city anticipated a famine.[178]

Raids continued along the Platte during july. Two emigrants were killed near Junction station on july 2. Six days later reports came by way of an Overland stage at Valley station that two men had been killed and scalped at Beaver creek, one mile above the station. A stage line horse, valued by the Holladay company at two hundred dollars, was taken by the Indians at Beaver creek on july 16. On the following day the station at Junction reported five of the stage horses taken from that point and eight from Murray, five stations eastward. Depredations on the Holladay line were very heavy from july 1864 to march 1865, with raids extending from northeastern Kansas through Nebraska territory to the northern part of Colorado territory. During that period, Holladay's losses were:

    37 stage horses by capture or death
  331 tons of hay
   55 sets of harness
3143 sacks of corn (each having a capacity of 112 pounds)

In addition to this, many dwelling houses, barns, corrals, warehouses, stations, stores, dishes and crockery, bedding, furniture, and clothing were taken,

---

[178] *Ibid.*, 406; Ware, *Indian war of 1864,* 197.

burned, or otherwise destroyed. In all, according to
the claims presented to the congressional committee
in 1880, Holladay lost $247,397.60 worth of property
from Indian depredations between july and march.
He also had claims amounting to $30,000.00 for stage
line property taken or used by United States soldiers
during 1864 and 1865, and claims of $31,000.00 for
Indian depredations during the spring and summer
of 1865. The grand total for property lost during
1864 and 1865 amounted to $309,147.60.

In august 1864 the Indians established a reign of
terror on the overland route near Fort Kearny. The
driver of a westbound coach arriving at the fort on
august 10 reported that no human beings or livestock
had been seen for fifty miles. A message from Omaha
said that an eastbound coach had brought news of the
burning of several trains and the death of eleven
people on the road. Six were killed at Thirty-two-
mile Creek, and livestock was taken at Cottonwood,
ninety miles west of Fort Kearny. Governor Evans
of Colorado territory called for volunteers to wage
war against the attackers. He asked all Indians who
were friendly to congregate at Forts Larned, Laramie, Lyons, and Camp Collins. An effort was also
made to stop transportation of mail between Fort
Kearny and a point forty miles west of Atchison. On
august 24 Denver reported that the western mail had
arrived on august 14 and no more mail-coaches were
expected for some time.[179] It was believed that four
thousand Indians were on the warpath. They formed

179 U.S. Senate. *Miscellaneous documents,* 46 cong., 2 sess., I, no. 19, 23-
88; *Report,* 46 cong., 2 sess., I, no. 216, 10-22; *Rocky mountain news* (Denver), july 18, 22, 1864.

into small parties, making swift raids, burning and pillaging. The white people along the overland route in Kansas, Nebraska and Colorado territories fled to the forts. Almost all travel had been suspended.[180]

On september 2 the acting second assistant post-master-general, E. L. Child, telegraphed the Denver postmaster to send all eastbound mail by way of San Francisco, where it could be carried by steamers to cities on the eastern coast. The order brought criticism of Holladay from a Denver newspaper. Holladay was said to have refused to restock the mail line until he should be given a new contract. The editor wrote:

. . . we hope that the contracts may be given first to someone to carry the mail with ox-teams if no better can be done. Ben Holladay seems to have obtained such complete control of all this western country that he can play with it as he pleases.

It was estimated that under the new service it would take thirty days to send mail from Denver to the east, with good connections. The acting postmaster at Denver, D. H. Moffatt jr., made a protest by wire to the second assistant postmaster-general against sending the mail by way of San Francisco. He thought that there was no just cause why Holladay should not carry the regular mails on his stage lines.

Major-general S. R. Curtis arrived at Fort Kearny on august 22 to gather troops for service against the Indians. The Pawnee tribe agreed to aid him. The Holladay stage line had moved agents, coaches, and

---

[180] Washington (D.C.) *daily national intelligencer,* september 7, 1864; *Rocky mountain news* (Denver), august 10-12, 24, 1864. Charts of depredations are given in appendix.

livestock on the eastern division to Fort Kearny for protection, and most of the white people between Omaha and Denver were gathered in two fortified posts, Columbus and Fort Curtis.

In the fall of 1864 it was reported that there were hostile savages extending over a region of four hundred miles between the Platte and the Arkansas. The soldiers were still too few in number to check the raiders. An exaggerated report from St. Louis said that two thousand people had been killed on the Platte and one hundred on the Arkansas and the Smoky Hill. It was also said that the property damage was three hundred thousand dollars, with five hundred mules, three thousand horses, and two thousand oxen captured. Troops at Fort Kearny, expecting an attack, prepared rifle pits and breastworks. Citizens in Kearney City built a round fortification in the middle of the town where they kept picket guards at night.

The Overland Stage line had discontinued its schedule entirely. Marysville, Kansas, estimated that five to eight thousand Indians were in that vicinity, mounted on fleet horses and supplied with good rifles and a provision train. At Latham on the South Platte seventy-five passengers and over one hundred sacks of mail were stalled. California mails had been sent eastward in august and september by way of the overland mail, but had been carried only a little beyond Denver and then returned. Patrons were being advised to mark all letters "per steamer" in order to have security for transportation.

Secretary of War Stanton was severely criticized

by one New York correspondent for his failure to protect the Overland route. The writer said that Holladay had called repeatedly for aid and that the postmaster-general had asked Stanton for troops. The line had, however, been unprotected for several hundred miles. Fort Kearny had sixty men, but what Holladay had requested was a guard of five men at each station. He had also offered to carry two soldiers in each coach to guard the mail if the government would supply them.[181]

On september 23 a stagecoach left Denver by way of the Platte route, bound for eastern points, and on september 26 McLellan, third assistant postmaster-general, ordered that the mail service to the west should be resumed by the Holladay lines. The first mail from the east reached Denver three days later. Because of the suspension of overland service, mail matter had accumulated at Atchison. Some had been rerouted to the east coast to be carried by boat to California, and on september 30 the steamer "Golden Age" brought to San Francisco over one hundred thousand delayed letters.

During this time Holladay's efforts to master the difficult Indian problem had been ceaseless. He had made several calls upon the postmaster-general and the president of the United States. President Lincoln was anxious concerning the mail service to the west, he feared that Confederate cruisers would hinder the Union mail steamers and insisted that the overland

181 Root and Connelley, *Overland stage,* 333; Washington (D.C.) *daily national intelligencer,* september 3, 1864; The Dalles (Oregon) *weekly mountaineer,* september 7, 1864; San Francisco *daily evening bulletin,* september 19, 20, 27, 1864.

service be maintained regardless of cost. Holladay explained that the mail contract would not pay him for the cost of forage and fuel along the lines under existing conditions, and that he must have passenger fares to escape financial ruin. Lincoln replied, "These are perilous times, Mr. Holladay, all over our country; my anxiety is great. We have no soldiers to spare, but I will do all in my power." In regard to what Holladay had said about his losses, Lincoln said reassuringly, "You will be reimbursed for all losses and damages; like all patriotic men, you must trust to the honor of our government." [182]

Colonel Chivington had telegraphed on september 22 to Secretary Stanton that he had a troop of one hundred men in the field but that they were delayed by Indians along the Platte. He said that the Indians held the road and had stopped the soldiers, so that he feared the short term of the soldiers would end before they reached Denver. On the same date Major-general Curtis reported that he had ordered a troop to Liberty Farm from Fort Kearny in order to speed plans for reestablishing the service. Holladay himself carried a message from Curtis to Colonel P. P. Livingston, asking him to help the troop with his own soldiers, and also consulted with him concerning the difficulties to be overcome. Curtis planned to establish strong military posts about fifty miles apart, with smaller outposts between these points. Soldiers were to act as escorts for persons and property moving along the route.

---

[182] *Ibid.*, september 30, 1864; Hafen, *Overland mail*, 261; U.S. Senate. *Miscellaneous documents*, 46 cong., 2 sess., I, no. 19, 62.

Holladay ordered his employees to bring the live-stock of the stage company from Kearney City under military escort. He was unable to hire any stock tenders at Kearney City and attempted to get them at Atchison. From that city, on september 23, he sent a message to Major-general Curtis at Fort Leavenworth, reporting that his paymaster had just reached Fort Kearny by way of the Little Blue river and had seen no Indians. He wrote, in part:

With your advice and my determination I know that we can put this line into operation so that there will be no interruption in this important service.

Curtis answered at once declaring that he wanted an early restoration of the mail service and would sacrifice protection on other routes, if necessary, to aid the Holladay road. He besought Holladay's patience and energy.

A ranch near Plum Creek was burned during the night of september 30. On the next day Holladay reported to Major-general Curtis from Julesburg that the Indians had resumed depredations by firing into coaches and into groups of haycutters on the Blue river. Fearing that his men would not stay at stations without military protection, he requested that five soldiers be placed at each station and that every coach have an escort of two soldiers so that the mail service could be kept open. On the same date Colonel Livingston sent word to General Curtis that he had seen Holladay. Livingston reported that he had stationed soldiers at Blue station, Pawnee ranch, Fort Kearny, Plum Creek, Midway, Cottonwood, O'Fallon's, Alkali, Beauvais, and Julesburg. Thus nine groups of soldiers were located west of Fort Kearny and one to the east. Livingston reported also that General Mitchell had arrived on september 28 and left two days later. Troops were stationed at Fort Cottonwood and soldiers had been distributed on the route between Cottonwood and Julesburg.

On october 10 Bela M. Hughes, Holladay's attorney, sent word from Atchison to General Curtis that Holladay had reached Salt Lake City after a narrow escape from the Indians. He protested against the defensive military policy of the government, saying that the Indians could attack stagecoaches and trains as soon as they were out of sight of the military posts. He urged a ruthless campaign during the winter to crush the enemy finally and effectually. On october 14 Colonel Chivington sent a message from Denver to Holladay at Salt Lake City reporting that his soldiers had killed twelve Indians in an engagement near Valley station.

Holladay was not satisfied with the work done by soldiers along his stage line. On october 15 he sent word from Salt Lake City to Secretary Stanton that Indians were attacking the mail-coaches every few days in the region extending fifty miles west of Fort Kearny. He asked for immediate aid and recommended the assignment of General Connor for that duty, since Connor's familiarity with Indian warfare had been proved by his past record. As the district around Salt Lake City was quiet at the time he felt that Connor could be spared for the campaign, which he believed should be carried on during the winter, when the pursuit of the Indians would be easier.[183]

On october 16 Major-general Halleck, chief of staff at Washington, D.C., ordered General Connor to give all possible protection to the stage route between Salt Lake City and Fort Kearny, without attention to departmental lines. Major-general Curtis was at this time engaged in a campaign against Confederate troops from Arkansas which were raiding Missouri.[184] General Connor requested that General Halleck make all troops on the overland lines subject to his orders. Halleck, however, merely asked the soldiers to cooperate with Connor.

About two weeks later Connor sent two hundred mounted soldiers from Camp Douglas to Fort Bridger. Connor himself rode to Denver on a Holladay coach to investigate conditions there. He was planning to use Denver as a base for the military campaign which was to be launched as soon as practicable. His hope was to secure a permanent peace by crushing the hostile Indians east of Denver.[185]

In the fall of 1864 Holladay was given a military order by Colonel Chivington which was hard to obey. He was told to move his stage line to the cut-off extending from Denver to Latham. Holladay protested vigorously against abandoning the old Platte river route at this time, as the fall season was almost over and all stations had been stocked with supplies for the winter. Grain sacks had been emptied into bins, employees had gone several hundred miles to refill

---

183 *War of the rebellion*, series I, XLI, part III, 313, 334, 549, 768, 877, 903.
184 *Ibid.*, series I, L, part II, 1013.
185 Coutant, *History of Wyoming*, I, 415.

the sacks with grain, and fuel was stored at the stations. The move, Holladay knew, would make it necessary to tear down the stations, haul them to the new route, and rebuild them.

The removal was made, but it occasioned a loss of hay, grain, and wood estimated at eighty thousand dollars. In addition to this the United States soldiers were said to have taken thirty thousand dollars worth of Holladay property. Under such trying circumstances the overland mail service continued, thanks to the wealth of Holladay, the strength of his resolution, and the courage of his employees.[186]

The Indians were becoming bolder late in october, and on the twenty-eighth of that month a party of haycutters working for Holladay at Midway station was attacked by some Pawnees. A troop of soldiers pursued the Indians, killing two and capturing three. On november 6 Indians attacked the Sand Hill stage station, but the Holladay guard of six men drove them off. A westbound coach near Plum Creek on november 25 was beset by Indians who wounded two passengers and cut the telegraph line. The *Black Hawk Mining Journal* reported that "painted hostiles" infested the overland route between Colorado territory and the states.

During the war of 1864 Holladay had lost a large amount of grain. One of his agents, George Henry Carlyle, later testified that about two hundred and fifty sacks of grain were destroyed at each station for a distance of three hundred miles, and an average of forty tons of hay was lost at each station. Even though

186 U.S. Senate. *Report,* 46 cong., 2 sess., I, no. 216, 9; *Miscellaneous documents,* I, no. 19, 2, 9, 53, 62, 63.

guards were sent from fifty to sixty miles with hay-cutters, some of the parties were killed by Indians.[187]

The unfortunate massacre of peaceful Indians at Sand creek, Colorado territory, increased the hostility of the red man. On november 29 they were attacked by Colonel Chivington's troops. In return mail-coaches were attacked and riddled with bullets and some of the drivers and passengers were scalped. All stations between Julesburg and Denver, with the exception of Hollen Godfrey's ranch, were burned by angry braves. Overland communication was halted for weeks and Denver faced a famine.

A complaint was made by a Black Hawk writer about the soldiers along the Platte route. They were likened to "straw men set up in a cornfield to scare away birds." The soldiers were said to have watched the raiding of trains and coaches and the killing of passengers but to have been unwilling to pursue the warriors. Although the country from Cottonwood to Kearney was full of Indians, the soldiers, it was reported, did not come near the white travelers until the attackers were a safe fifteen miles away. A request was made for the return of Colorado troops to insure better protection.[188]

On january 1, 1865, Major-general Curtis at Fort Leavenworth telegraphed Holladay at New York that although the Indians were reported to be holding the line from Julesburg to Valley station near Denver he would take over Julesburg and the entire overland

---

[187] *Ibid.*, I, no. 19, 37; Black Hawk (Colo. terr.) *mining journal,* december 6, 1864.

[188] *Ibid.*, december 7, 1864; Coutant, *History of Wyoming,* I, 418, 419; Parsons, *Making of Colorado,* 199, 200.

line if possible. During the same week Valley station was burned, and five miles from the station seventy-five savages killed twelve men and burned their wagons. The coaches from Denver turned back at this point.[189]

On january 7 one thousand Cheyennes, Sioux, and Arapahoes attacked Julesburg. They chased a stage-coach from a point four miles east of Julesburg to Benton's ranch, two miles farther on, and fired into it without causing any serious damage. The coach later proceeded to Julesburg where horses were changed. At Fort Rankin, one mile west of Julesburg, the driver of the coach asked for a military escort, but Captain N. J. O'Brien was unable to furnish the soldiers, and the coach returned to Julesburg. Leading a group from the Seventh Iowa cavalry, Captain O'Brien pursued a few Indians who retreated to the south. A larger body of Indians almost cut off the soldiers from the fort before they could escape. Fifteen soldiers were killed in the fight.

During the battle at Julesburg its inhabitants fled to Fort Rankin. The Indians then took possession of the town for about an hour. Bedding, clothing, flour, sugar, and other provisions were seized and the telegraph office was destroyed. One list of losses read as follows:

ARTICLES	VALUE
Two bales of clothing	$1500
One mule	$ 200
One coach, damaged	$ 500

---

[189] Grinnell, *The fighting Cheyennes,* 180; *Rocky mountain news* (Denver), january 7, 1865; Black Hawk (Colo. terr.) *mining journal,* january 10, 1865.

The Indians smashed all windows, doors, and furniture in the town and robbed the stagecoach. One box of greenbacks, however, was carried by the messenger to Fort Rankin before the warriors arrived. Two days later another stage messenger found a treasure trunk containing some money about two miles from Julesburg. Richard Quinn, local agent for the Holladay line at Julesburg, reported the destruction of seven sacks of mail.[190]

Upon receiving a report from Captain O'Brien that there were four thousand Indians on the Republican river and that four men had been killed at Dennison's ranch, General Mitchell, commander of the Platte department, proceeded to collect the soldiers from the Holladay line at Camp Cottonwood. From that point, on january 16, he sent about five hundred cavalrymen to the scene of destruction. No Indians were found along the Republican river, and the expedition returned ten days later. The situation grew more alarming. Two thousand Cheyennes, Sioux, and Arapahoes were reported to be operating near Julesburg and about the same number near Fort Kearny. A large number of Kiowas and Comanches were said to be moving northward from the Arkansas river. On january 28 the Indians struck again and destroyed almost one hundred miles of the stage route above and below Julesburg. Ranches and stations were burned and livestock captured. All ranches between Julesburg and Valley station were destroyed. When news of the raid spread, stagecoaches stopped running.

190 *Ibid.*, january 13, 1865; *Rocky mountain news* (Denver), january 9, 1865; U.S. Senate. *Miscellaneous documents,* 46 cong., 2 sess., I, no. 19, 25, 28, 29.

Colonel Thomas C. Moonlight, Eleventh Kansas cavalry, had reported the serious state of affairs to the legislature at Golden City and had threatened the use of martial law and draft if there were no legislative action, but still nothing was being done to provide better means for raising troops.[191]

The Indians returned to Julesburg on february 2, 1865. About fifteen hundred of them took possession of the town. Although there was great destruction, the soldiers at Fort Rankin, watching the raid, did not interfere. There were losses of livestock, grain, hay, stores, and buildings. Much of the property was burned. Bela M. Hughes later estimated that the buildings at Julesburg had been worth at least thirty-five thousand dollars. Planks and shingles used in their construction had been hauled from Denver, one hundred and eighty miles, and some of the logs had come from Cottonwood, one hundred miles away. Holladay's claims for damages from the raid amounted to one hundred seventeen thousand three hundred dollars.[192]

Holladay also suffered losses of property from Indian raids elsewhere in january. The Beaver Creek stage station had been burned on january 14 and the Spring Hill station was destroyed fourteen days later.

---

[191] Grinnell, *The fighting Cheyennes*, 180-182; *Rocky mountain news* (Denver), january 7, 1865; Black Hawk (Colo. terr.) *mining journal*, january 10, 11, february 1, 1865. Fort Rankin was established in august 1864 near Julesburg, Colorado territory.

[192] U.S. Senate. *Miscellaneous documents*, 46 cong., 2 sess., I, no. 19, 27, 30, 87, 88; Grinnell, *The fighting Cheyennes*, 184, 185. The hay was valued at fifty dollars a ton and the corn at twenty cents a pound; the buildings consisted of shops, barns, warehouses, corrals, telegraph offices, and dwellings.

Planters Hotel, Holladay Station, Denver

The latter was said by Hughes to be one of the best on the line, with excellent horses, barns, and corrals. It was a home station, valued at six thousand dollars. On january 14 the American ranch had been burned by one hundred Indians, who also raided Godfrey's ranch. Wagon-trains in the vicinity were attacked and several men were killed. On january 28, six hundred and fifty cattle had been taken near Valley station and one hundred tons of hay had been burned.

Early in february the Holladay line presented a sad spectacle. Scattered along the road near Julesburg were dead livestock and Indians and the graves of whites. At American ranch two hundred and fifty head of livestock had been lost, and at Julesburg thirty-seven wagon-loads of corn and flour had been scattered and destroyed. At Gillette's ranch seventeen wagons filled with six hundred sacks of government flour had been lost. The road between Julesburg and Junction was held by Cheyennes, Sioux, and Arapahoes. Mail service had been checked.[193]

With the stations and forage between Denver and Julesburg destroyed, Holladay tried to secure forage in february from Major-general John Pope, commander of the division of the Missouri at St. Louis, but he found that all government forage was needed by the military forces. Pope assured Holladay that his troops would protect the overland route in the future, but advised him to put his mail and main stations at military posts. Advice and promises were poor

---

[193] Black Hawk (Colo. terr.) *mining journal,* february 9, 14, 22, 1865; *Rocky mountain news* (Denver), january 16, 17, 28, 1865; U.S. Senate. *Miscellaneous documents,* 46 cong., 2 sess., I, no. 19, 30, 87, 88.

consolation for Holladay at a time when his property lay in ruins and his animals were going unfed. Nevertheless, he carried on.

When the service had been stopped late in january, mail had accumulated in Denver. On february 3 eighty sacks of mail were sent eastward from Denver in five stagecoaches under an escort of forty soldiers. Colonel Moonlight put the Denver district under martial law five days later and raised soldiers to protect the stage line from Denver to Julesburg. The regular coach schedule was in operation at Denver on march 8. By that time new troops had been placed on the route. On february 20 the Eleventh Kansas cavalry left Fort Riley under Colonel P. B. Plumb and received equipment at Fort Kearny. They marched to Fort Laramie and were distributed along the Holladay line. Posts such as Horseshoe Creek, La Bonta, Deer Creek, and Platte Bridge had troops to be used for Indian patrol and for escort duty.[194]

The troops on the Overland Stage line in april were distributed as follows:

COMPANIES	ORGANIZATION	LOCATION
A,E,F,H,I,K	First Nebraska cavalry veteran volunteers	near Cottonwood Springs
C	First Nebraska cavalry veteran volunteers	Fort Kearny
G	First Nebraska cavalry veteran volunteers	Plum Creek
D	First battalion Nebraska veteran cavalry	Omaha

[194] Kansas state historical society *collections,* VIII, 353; *Rocky mountain news* (Denver), february 3, 6, 13, 1865; *War of the rebellion,* series I, XLVIII, part I, 997.

COMPANIES	ORGANIZATION	LOCATION
A,C	First battalion Nebraska veteran cavalry	near Cottonwood Springs
B	First battalion Nebraska veteran cavalry	Dakota City
A,B,C,F	Seventh Iowa cavalry	near Cottonwood Springs
E	Seventh Iowa cavalry	Columbus
A,D,I,L	Eleventh Ohio cavalry volunteers	Fort Laramie
C	Eleventh Ohio cavalry volunteers	Fremont's Orchard
H	Eleventh Ohio cavalry volunteers	Camp Mitchell
B,F	Eleventh Ohio cavalry volunteers	Camp Collins [195]

In an endeavor to keep the stagecoaches operating, in march General Grenville F. Dodge ordered General Mitchell at Omaha to allow the Holladay company corn for feed if it could possibly be spared. Escorts were also to be provided for the coaches. On march 28 he suggested the organization of a department of the Plains, under which were to be placed the districts of Colorado, Nebraska, and Utah. Denver was to be the base. Brigadier-general Connor was asked to command the department. The names of General Lew Wallace and B. F. Butler were also mentioned for the place, but the choice of Connor was approved by General U. S. Grant and General Halleck.

The plan for the department of the Plains failed to materialize. Instead the department of Missouri was

[195] Coutant, *History of Wyoming*, I, 432.

extended to include Nebraska territory, Kansas, and
Colorado territory. Major-general Pope, with headquarters at St. Louis, was assigned the command,
while General Connor was made responsible for the
protection of the overland route throughout the west.
Connor was given headquarters at Denver and was
promised an ample amount of troops for his work.
Two thousand cavalrymen and four hundred pack
mules were assigned to him for a campaign against
the Indians in the Powder river region. Infantry was
to replace cavalry so that the mail route could be
maintained against all dangers.

It was a source of gratification to business men in
the east, who had relations with California, that the
stage line was to be reopened. Holladay had announced the date as march 15, but it was april before
General Connor sent forth the word that it was safe
to start overland service. Carter, agent at Fort Bridger, then asked the San Francisco agent to commence
sending eastern mails by the regular schedule.[196]

The suspension of service on the overland line had
brought severe criticism to Senator John Conness of
California. Conness had denounced the mail contractors, claiming the stories of Indian hostilities in
the west to be fabrications, and saying that the only
Indians along the route were a few braves hired by
Holladay to create a stir whenever he wanted a new
mail contract. He had expressed these beliefs before
McLellan, now second assistant postmaster-general,

---

196 Coutant, *History of Wyoming*, I, 448; San Francisco *daily evening
bulletin*, march 3, 14, april 8, 1865; Tullidge, *History of Salt Lake City*, I,
178; *Omaha weekly herald*, february 17, 1865; *Army and navy journal*,
II, 502.

and General Craig, who in deference to his wishes had not taken the needed steps toward protecting the route. Conness's dislike for the Wells, Fargo company, owners of an interest in the mail contract, had been largely responsible for his attempt to prevent the assignment of soldiers to the work at a time when there had been several hundred of them idle at Fort Leavenworth. It was this lack of protection, brought about partly through Conness's personal enmity, which invited the angry Indians to commit depredations as Holladay had predicted.

Every tribe, from the headwaters of the Missouri to Texas, appeared in the spring and summer of 1865 to have commenced merciless depredations against the white man. Troops were assembled at Fort Laramie for infantry duty along the mail route. Others were assigned to scout and escort duty. The Nebraska veteran volunteer cavalry, the Sixth Michigan cavalry, and the Sixteenth Kansas volunteers all performed this type of service. The number of soldiers was still far from adequate, and better equipment was needed.

On may 8 one hundred hostile Indians, possibly Cheyennes, attacked three men driving wagons near Fort Laramie, killing one of the men and taking the wagons. Some stagecoach passengers reported at Atchison that Indians had raided Mulhally station about fifty miles west of Fort Kearny and captured four horses. The warriors had been driven off by troops, but the coach had been delayed for three hours, after which an escort had guarded the coach from Valley station to Fort Kearny. A few days later another Holladay coach was attacked along the Little Blue river and was chased for six miles. Two soldiers were killed and several wounded. A coach was also attacked four miles east of Pawnee station and followed to Buffalo Spring ranch.[197] During may troops from Fort Bridger were active doing escort duty and pursuing Indians. On may 28 fifty-one men of Company A and forty men of Company B, First Nebraska volunteer cavalry, were sent from the fort to pursue marauders. In june troops from the army posts continued their services along the stage route.

Despite these conditions, Speaker Schuyler Colfax and his party showed no fear of traveling on the Holladay line. They set off in may across the devastated Indian country by stagecoach. Four soldiers regularly acted as escorts during most of the trip, although six were on guard as the stage rolled westward from Fort Bridger. The travelers were fortunate in encountering no Indians, but they saw enough to convince them that Indians were dangerously near. Word reached them of depredations west of Virginia Dale station, where Indians had driven away the livestock from three stations. They passed on the road the bodies of two emigrants who had been killed by arrows and scalped. Thirty minutes after the coach had left Willow Springs the station was attacked, and on the following day Sage Creek station was raided after the Colfax party had passed. Many of the stone stations on their way had loopholes in the walls for defense purposes. They witnessed, too, an unsuccessful

197 Atchison (Kans.) *daily free press,* may 13, 22, 1865; Camp Douglas (Utah terr.) *daily union vedette,* may 9, 1865; Sacramento *daily union,* april 19, 1865; San Francisco *daily evening bulletin,* april 6, 9, 12, 1865.

attack by Indians upon an emigrant train. There was no doubt in their minds, after this trip, that Senator Conness had been wrong in estimating the menace of the Indian.[198]

On may 11 General Connor moved his headquarters from Denver to Julesburg. He ordered Colonel Moonlight at Fort Laramie to distribute two companies of the Third United States volunteers along the North Platte to Sweetwater and westward to South pass. It was necessary to protect the stage crossing at Laramie plains as well as the telegraph lines in that region.

In june the Indians were active between Virginia Dale and Fort Halleck. The Holladay company was forced to abandon many stations, and concentrated its livestock at Big Laramie and Fort Halleck. On june 4 fourteen horses were taken at Fort Halleck. It was reported that over six hundred Indians were on the overland route near-by. When the Willow Springs station was robbed in june and the Sage Creek station was burned, two employees of Sage Creek station and three soldiers were killed in the fight and twenty mules and ten horses were lost. Two men escaped. Fifteen head of livestock were taken from Elk Mountain station during the latter part of june. The Holladay line also lost eighty-seven head of livestock between Cherokee and Sulphur Springs station, and soldiers at four stations lost their horses. Indians were repulsed in their attack on Cooper's Creek.

Because of the scarcity of livestock, stages began to

198 *Ibid.*, august 8, 1865; Richardson, *Beyond the Mississippi*, 327, 328, 338; Post returns Fort Bridger, may, june, 1865, MS. (War department, old records division, Washington, D.C.).

run tri-weekly.[199] General Connor, at Julesburg, reported on june 12 that the Indians were quiet on the road east from Denver and that four companies of the Eleventh Kansas cavalry had left Fort Laramie to protect the line west of North Platte. Orders were sent to Fort Bridger to distribute troops along the route. Company B, with sixty men from Company C, First battalion, Nevada cavalry, was sent to Waskie station. Headquarters was established there, with thirty men on duty, and groups of five soldiers each were placed at Rock Springs, Salt Wells, Rock Point, Black Buttes, and Big Pond. In addition, fifteen soldiers were sent to Laclede and similar groups were placed at Duck Springs and Duck Lake.

Throughout the summer the depredations continued. Passengers congregated at Denver, Fort Halleck, and Fort Bridger, fearful of encountering Indians along the route. By july 15 a new brigade of soldiers was near Julesburg to give further protection, but the line between Julesburg and Fort Laramie was reported to be menaced during the latter part of july by attempts to drive off livestock. During the months of june and july many had lost their lives between Denver and Julesburg, and approximately seventy-five white persons had been killed between Big Laramie and Bridger Pass stations.

Reports were often contradictory. On july 26 it was reported that the Platte river route was quiet, but soon word came that the Sixteenth Kansas cavalry had lost six horses along the river. Scattered reports came in: that fifteen soldiers had been chased thirty miles

---

199 Coutant, *History of Wyoming*, I, 445, 447, 452, 455; *Rocky mountain news* (Denver), june 17, 26, 1865.

to Valley station; that Dennison's ranch late in july had suffered the loss of two men; that travel on the Pole creek route was to be resumed at the traveler's own risk.

By attacking wagon-trains, small parties of soldiers, ranches, stations, and coaches, the Indians were rapidly accumulating more arms and supplies. There was a method in this arming. They had resented General Connor's expedition to the Powder river region, and early in august they retaliated by attacking the entire route between Big Laramie and Rock Creek. Little Laramie station on the Laramie plains was raided and burned. This was a home station built of hewn logs and consisting of one house with stove and furniture, a corral, and a stable, and was valued at thirty-five hundred dollars. Antelope station, one of the swing type, was also destroyed in the raid. With its house, barn and corral it was valued at two to three thousand dollars.[200]

Holladay continued to suffer losses at the hands of the United States soldiers. George Otis, a Holladay official, later testified that between october 1864 and december 1865 they had damaged the line to the extent of thirty thousand dollars. The records were not exact, as many stage line employees had failed to keep accounts. The troops and government agents were alleged to have taken and used hay, grain, and other supplies without giving Holladay any compensation. Carlyle testified that twenty-nine head of

[200] *Ibid.,* june 12, 20, july 26, 31, august 10, 1865; Coutant, *op. cit.,* I, 445, 447, 452, 453, 462, 491, 492; Camp Douglas (Utah terr.) *daily union vedette,* june 14, 1865; U.S. Senate. *Miscellaneous documents,* 46 cong., 2 sess., I, no. 19, 44, 87.

oxen, valued at one hundred dollars each, were taken at one time from Fort Kearny, and that one hundred cords of wood were taken by soldiers from Julesburg.

While the west was concerning itself with Indian wars the Civil war in the south and east had ended in may. When the news reached them many of the soldiers along the overland route expected to be mustered out of service at once. General Connor, however, believed that the men were still needed. Companies of the First Nebraska and Eleventh Kansas cavalry led in the demand for discharge. As these companies had not seen much service in the protection of the stage line it was not until august, when Colonel Peter S. Stagg's First Michigan veteran cavalry arrived in the west, that they were relieved.[201]

There seems to have been an erroneous impression abroad that United States soldiers carried the mail. Bob Spotswood, superintendent of the Overland Stage line, in a later report of the summer's activities, explained that although the soldiers acted as escorts for the coaches they were not a part of the mail service. Spotswood himself had hauled the mail in an army ambulance on june 15 from Sulphur Springs to Fort Halleck, using two government mules and four belonging to Holladay. The next day from seventy-five to one hundred Indians had made a raid at Sulphur Springs, capturing the stage livestock and escaping pursuit by the station guard, four soldiers, James Stewart (another Holladay agent), and him-

---

[201] *Ibid.*, I, no. 19, 58; Barnes, *From Atlantic to Pacific*, 25; Post returns Fort Bridger, july 1865, MS. (War department, old records division, Washington, D.C.); Coutant, *History of Wyoming*, I, 463, 489; U.S. Senate. *Report*, 46 cong., 2 sess., I, no. 216, 11.

self. Stewart had lost forty-five head of livestock,
Spotswood six mules and a saddle horse. All the livestock, except two government mules, had been owned
by Holladay. Spotswood said that the mail had run
daily over the route between Denver and Virginia
Dale, as there was no trouble from Indians in that
vicinity, but that the division between Virginia Dale
and North Platte was beset with danger. He had ordered the drivers of mail-coaches to drive the one
hundred and twenty-six miles during the night hours
and to hide in the day-time in some high place from
which the surrounding territory could be watched.
For forty-five miles Stewart's division had been
broken by Indians, and Spotswood had taken the
mails across the break to meet Stewart and the government escort.

Holladay's losses from Indian raids between Denver and Green River amounted to thirty thousand
eight hundred dollars. Some of these were:

65 horses	1 bull
7 ponies	8 cows
46 mules	2 yoke of oxen
11 sets of harness damaged or stolen	

Windows, furniture, and corrals were destroyed.
Holladay was busy replacing livestock and rebuild-
ing stations between Virginia Dale and Sulphur
Springs. Depredations were so common that it was
difficult to keep a sufficient number of animals to haul
the stagecoaches.[202]

Two employees were killed in a raid at Sage Creek

---

[202] *Ibid.*, I, no. 216, 17, 18; *Miscellaneous documents,* 46 cong., 2 sess., I,
no. 19, 30, 33, 34, 44, 45.

on september 4 and the station and barn were destroyed. However, conditions in general had improved by that time. General Connor's military expedition to the Powder river region had reached the home lands of the Sioux, Cheyenne, and Arapahoe tribes. The warriors, returning to protect their lodges, disappeared for a few weeks from the overland route. Stagecoaches continued to go under escort, but by september 12 they began running on daily schedule instead of semi-weekly between Denver and Salt Lake City.

Mail had been suspended for three weeks in august. General Connor, absent on the Powder river campaign, gave his assistant orders which insured the daily service. Officers were advised to stay on the trail of the hostile Indians until they were punished. Soldiers were to protect the mail and telegraph routes, and to have available at all times twenty-day rations to be used during the pursuit of the enemy, together with an extra ration of salt for the preservation of game on the march. This "war to the knife" policy caused amusement among newspaper editors. The Indians had put up a strong front, and to the commentators it was not credible that the soldiers could catch and punish them within the twenty days for which rations were provided. It was hinted that the government would need to use that salt many times before the campaign was over. The suggestion was made that the government give the soldiers a course in the proper salting of meat before sending them in pursuit of the wily enemy. One cartoon of the day pictured soldiers hanging to the north pole, complaining that after following the Indian trail to that point they were short of food because the polar bears in the vicinity refused to wait and be salted.

General Connor's policy was sound, however. While some of the soldiers were in the field for the purpose of menacing the war bands near the stage-coach route, others were being used to protect the property. Mail escorts, under his plan, were composed of at least four soldiers, more if necessary, and were supposed to keep within three hundred yards of the stagecoach. The Sixth Michigan volunteer cavalry and the Eleventh Ohio cavalry under Major George A. Drew were very busy during the month of october escorting mail-coaches in the vicinity of Fort Laramie.[203]

General Connor's military expedition to the north was ordered to return to Fort Laramie in october. Four battles had been fought, and four or five hundred Indians and twenty-five of Connor's men had been killed. The Arapahoe village was destroyed. Five hundred horses and mules, as well as five hundred cattle were captured, but there was also a loss to the military forces of about six hundred horses and two hundred mules during the campaign. As had happened before, thorough conquest of the tribes was prevented by the fact that the army horses were too exhausted after battle to pursue the Indians, and they could return to menace stagecoach travel.

[203] Gold Hill (Nevada terr.) *daily news,* september 12, 1865; Camp Douglas (Utah terr.) *daily union vedette,* september 8, 11, 1865; Post returns Fort Laramie, september 1865, MS. (War department, old records division, Washington, D.C.); *Rocky mountain news* (Denver), september 1, 1865.

On october 19 a coach left Denver carrying Holladay's attorney, Hughes, and five other passengers.
The coach messenger was in charge of two hundred
fifty thousand dollars in treasure. Twice in the region
of O'Fallon's Bluffs the coach was attacked, but each
time escape to a near-by station was effected and a
successful defense made. During the second attack
two companies of West Virginia cavalry arrived in
time to save the party.[204]

On october 24, General Pope, commander of the
department of Missouri, sent a telegram to General
Grant, asking if mounted escorts for stagecoaches had
still to be provided, as it would necessitate the for-
warding of a constant supply of horses as well as an
increased number of soldiers. Pope thought that the
stage company should provide its own guards. General Grant replied, "You need not furnish escorts to
the Overland stages except when it can be done without inconvenience or expense." He added that the
route should be protected as well as possible, and that
when soldiers were being transferred along the route
troops should move with the coaches. He suggested
also that, since regular soldiers were now being ordered westward, General Pope should muster the
volunteers out of service.

As a result of the new arrangement, about the
middle of november four regiments were at St. Louis
en route to the west to protect the overland line. In
the opinion of one Salt Lake City writer these soldiers would have "less effect than a flea," and travel-

---

[204] *Army and navy journal*, III, 17, 82, 98; Coutant, *History of Wyoming*, I, 500, 501.

ers could still expect no security from the Indians.[205]

Throughout the fall Indian raids continued. On october 28 warriors raided Alkali station. They attacked a wagon-train and killed four men, looting the wagons and destroying everything they were unable to carry away. Troops under General Herman H. Heath commenced pursuit and engaged in two victorious battles with three hundred Indians on Stinking Water, killing twenty-nine. Across the river five Indians were reported to have followed a coach for ten miles. On november 7, seven hundred warriors pursued a stage into Cottonwood station and surrounded the post. A few days later Indians took ten head of livestock from Pole Cat station. Horseshoe station, fifty miles east of Fort Laramie, was attacked on november 26 and thirty head of livestock were taken.

Secretary Stanton continued to receive his share of criticism for not sufficiently punishing the Indians when thousands of people were losing millions of dollars worth of property, to say nothing of the loss in human life. The recalling of troops from the plains had stimulated hostile activity.[206] In november Colonel Stagg of the First Michigan veteran cavalry brought new troops from the east to Fort Bridger. He assumed command of the post and retained four companies of the former garrison from the First battalion, Nevada volunteers. On november 16 he sent two companies of that troop to Camp Douglas.

---

[205] *Ibid.*, I, 502; Camp Douglas (Utah terr.) *daily union vedette,* november 20, 1865.

[206] *Ibid.*, november 7, 21, 30, 1865; Omaha *weekly herald,* november 10, 17, 1865; Atchison (Kans.) *daily free press,* november 3, 9, 1865.

At Fort Laramie late in november soldiers were
sent out in pursuit of Indians said to be committing
depredations forty miles north of the post, but the
troop's horses became exhausted by the chase and the
Indians escaped. In december Fort Laramie, under
Colonel H. E. Maynadier, had nine companies, three
hundred and forty men at the post. The Sixth United
States volunteers, Seventh Iowa, Twelfth Missouri,
and Eleventh Ohio troops were stationed there for
escort duty.[207]

No matter how menacing the Indian may have
appeared at the time, he was fighting a losing battle.
As soldiers were released from duty in the eastern
part of the country an increasing number were being
sent west. Holladay's difficulties, however, were not
completely eased by this hopeful prospect, because
at this time he had decided to take over another stagecoach route with its attendant Indian problems. He
purchased the Butterfield Overland Despatch, which
ran a stagecoach line over the Smoky Hill route.

On march 31, 1866, he announced that the Holladay Overland Mail and Express company would be
ready on april 15 to furnish daily connection with the
Union Pacific railroad by way of the Smoky Hill
route to Denver. Coaches were placed on the line to
carry mail, express, treasure, and passengers.[208]

Before Holladay became owner of the Butterfield
overland stage route it had suffered from Indian

207 Post returns Fort Laramie, november, december, 1865; Fort Bridger,
november 1865, MS. (War department, old records division, Washington,
D.C.).

208 Wilder, *Annals of Kansas*, 437; Junction City (Kans.) *union*, april
7, 1866; Atchison (Kans.) *daily free press*, january 29, 1866.

raids, but he knew that the Indians, not wanting to be caught between the strong line of troops along the Platte and Arkansas rivers, were fewer along this way than they were on his main line. In may, however, word had come that two hundred Cheyennes were at Limestone creek, about seventy miles above the mouth of the Solomon river. They had killed an old settler and driven some white hunters down the stream under forced escort. Settlers in the region had brought their families to Fort Solomon, where troops had been organized to pursue the warriors.

The Ogallala Sioux now asked the Pawnees to surrender all lands between the Platte and the Arkansas, which they claimed for themselves. The southern Cheyennes had formed a confederation with the Sioux, and the united tribes protested the development of a stagecoach line through their best buffalo country. Lieutenant Julian R. Fitch had explored the Smoky Hill region for the Butterfield company during the summer of 1864, and reported that the country near Fort Ellsworth was black with buffalo peacefully grazing on fine grass. He estimated that he had seen a million buffalo there, although it was the belief of experts that the number was even greater. It was not surprising that the Indian, to whom the buffalo was both food and shelter, objected to the appropriation of his hunting ground.[209]

With the added opposition of Indians along the Platte river and in Kansas, United States government

---

[209] Ware, *Indian war of 1864*, 260, 586; Junction City (Kans.) *union*, may 19, 1866. See also Fitch, "Report" in Trails clippings (Library of Kansas state historical society) I, 374.

officials had been influenced to listen to peace over-
tures. The Sioux and Cheyennes had sent messengers
to Fort Laramie in february 1866 to arrange for a
peace council. The request materialized into fact at
Fort Laramie on june 1, when the United States com-
missioners, E. B. Taylor, Superintendent Henry E.
Maynadier, also commander of the fort, R. M. Mc-
Claren, and Thomas Wister assembled to meet delegates from the hostile Indian tribes. Congress had
appropriated twenty thousand dollars for the peace
negotiations, and many gifts were on hand for the
Indians. Three thousand of them came to the meeting, and the fort issued rations until its supply was
almost exhausted. Between may 1 and may 14 the following supplies were issued:

15,315 pounds shoulders	2,875 pounds hominy
100 pounds bacon	4,000 pounds peas
83,714 pounds fresh beef	640 pounds green coffee
575 pounds flour	687 pounds roasted coffee
30,085 pounds hard bread	4,227 pounds sugar
10 pounds rice	547 pounds salt
20 pounds soap (used to tan skins)	

At the council the Indians demanded the withdrawal
of all troops and all travel from their hunting
grounds. A compromise was made whereby the northern Cheyennes and Arapahoes agreed to allow travel
on the Bozeman road between Platte Bridge and
Bozeman in Montana territory. Fourteen chiefs
signed the document.

The Sioux were not so easily pacified. Their noted
chief, Red Cloud, mustered three hundred braves to
obstruct the enforcement of the treaty. They began

further depredations near Fort Reno in Dakota territory, and in an effort to control the Indians to the north of the overland route the government established Fort Philip Kearny.[210] Reports concerning the comparative failure of the Laramie peace council reached the east, where it was now called a "complete farce." On august 14 Fort Kearny heard that the Indian war had broken out again in full force around Laramie. A wagon-train had been captured between Forts Reno and Laramie, and the livestock from the train had been taken into the mountains. Indians had also captured three herds of cattle near Fort Laramie. Several white men were killed near Fort Reno and three persons were shot by arrows near Alkali.

The Indians in Kansas had continued depredations during the month of july. On july 11, 1866, a white man was killed near Little Blue station. Cheyennes in that region were stealing livestock, burning abandoned houses, and killing all white men who had not fled up the river for safety. Ten thousand warriors were reported to have returned from Laramie, and it was said that they had a large supply of arms and ammunition to use against the few soldiers remaining in the region. All persons crossing the plains were warned to be prepared to meet "these red villains which the United States government has just been paying for committing depredations on us." Eight hundred Pawnees and Omahas killed seven surveyors and drove settlers from the forks of the Solomon river.

[210] Bancroft, *History of Nevada, Colorado, Wyoming*, 716-719; *Rocky mountain news* (Denver), june 10, 1866; San Francisco *daily evening bulletin*, august 16, 1866.

The state of Kansas, aroused by these hostilities, planned a campaign against the Indians. Governor Samuel J. Crawford ordered General W. F. Cloud to the frontier with full power to enroll men and officers for the purpose of protecting settlers.[211] In september the United States soldiers went into action. The Third United States cavalry, consisting of about four hundred soldiers, arrived at Fort Leavenworth on september 1 en route to the west to protect the Smoky Hill route. General Winfield S. Hancock ordered out one hundred men from Fort Ellsworth and a company from Fort Kearny to scout the country for Indians. General Cloud of the Kansas troops sent an officer to the Pawnee, Otoe, and Omaha reservations to demand indemnity for outrages. It was believed that a fort on the Solomon river would be added protection, but General William T. Sherman, to whom the request was sent, refused to take such action, offering instead the suggestion that Governor Crawford of Kansas call out two thousand volunteers to join a few regular soldiers under the leadership of United States army officers. Governor Crawford refused to support the idea.[212]

The warriors continued to harass the overland stage line, with the result that the military forces retreated to stockades which had been built upon a part of the route along the Platte. Deer Creek station, ninety

211 *Ibid.*, august 8, 1866; Central City (Colo. terr.) *daily miner's register*, july 10, 1866; Topeka *tribune*, august 31, 1866; Atchison (Kans.) *daily free press*, july 10, 15, 1866; Omaha *weekly herald*, august 17, 1866; Marysville (Kans.) *enterprise*, july 28, 1866.

212 *Ibid.*, september 1, 1866; Junction City (Kans.) *union*, september 1, 1866.

miles west of Fort Laramie, was burned and the telegraph wires were torn down. Near Wagon Pound
ninety head of oxen were taken. Three hundred
young Cheyennes, called "dog soldiers" attacked the
Chalk Bluffs station on the Smoky Hill route about
two hundred miles east of Denver. Two Holladay
stock tenders were killed. Other Holladay employees
deserted the station to join some soldiers who were
on the march westward, and two weeks later the "dog
soldiers" returned to burn the station. On august 30
Fremont Springs was raided by Indians believed to
be Sioux, who drove off twelve head of livestock,
seven of which belonged to Holladay. The employees
of Miller's ranch near Plum Creek were compelled
to furnish tobacco and other articles to sixty armed
Sioux from the Republican river. Indians near Julesburg drove off ninety-six mules from the train of
Holladay's freighter, Carlyle, and also drove off one
hundred and fifty cattle owned by a Denver firm. The
report of Street, general agent for the stage line, said
that the capture was made twelve miles east of Fort
Sedgewick, and that it was believed the attackers were
Sioux. Depredations were committed and travelers
imperiled at other points. Companies K and M of the
Second United States cavalry engaged one group of
braves, losing two soldiers, killing five Indians, and
wounding fifteen. Pursuit of other warring parties
failed.[213]

---

[213] Omaha *weekly herald,* september 7, october 12, 1866; San Francisco
daily evening bulletin, september 13, october 5, 11, november 19, 1866;
Rocky mountain news (Denver), august 30, october 18, 1866; U.S. Department of interior, office of Indian affairs, commissioner's *report,* upper
Arkansas agency, 1866.

Despite conditions Holladay continued to push his stage line activities. The requirement that emigrant trains have an escort of thirty armed men was delaying his business. There was no time, under existing circumstances, to wait for such protection to be provided, and he endeavored to have the requirement set aside. Emigrant trains continued to obey it, but Holladay, by assuming all risks, was able to send his wagon-trains, loaded with supplies and equipment for his stage line, through the danger zones.

On october 23, 1866, Chauncey McKeever, assistant adjutant-general at St. Louis, wrote Holladay at Denver, saying that he was ready to do everything possible to protect the mail route. He asserted, however, that he needed more troops and that it was too late in the season to establish any new posts other than Camp Fletcher at Big Creek. His plan was to have at each station two or three horses, forage, a cart to haul wood, subsistence for two months, and sufficient ammunition. Escorts were to be furnished daily, or whenever the mail-coaches should arrive. The following troops were to be stationed on the route:

Three of infantry and two of cavalry at Fort Ellsworth
Two of infantry and one of cavalry at Big Creek (Camp Fletcher)
Two of infantry and one of cavalry at Fort Wallace
Two of infantry and one of cavalry at Fort Morgan

The Seventh company at Fort Riley was expected to furnish troops for Forts Ellsworth and Wallace and to Camp Fletcher, but lacked sufficient horses and had no commanding officer at the time. The soldiers assigned to duty were to be ordered not to interfere with the stage company's officers and employees.[214]

Holladay's efforts to secure protection during the years of Indian depredations were not confined to his main line. Although his losses were not so great on the stage roads of Montana and Idaho territories, nevertheless he had a problem to meet there also. The Snake Indian tribe was a great source of danger to Montana stage travel. Its members were fierce and crafty fighters, at home in the rough mountainous country. The Indian tribes of Idaho territory also actively resented intrusion on their home lands. Fort Hall was insufficient protection for the branch stage line, since after 1860 the government had kept troops there only at irregular intervals. When in 1865 the fort had become almost a mass of ruins, soldiers took material from it as well as from abandoned buildings of the Overland Stage company and built Camp Lander at the junction of the Salt Lake City–Virginia City–Boise City roads, three miles east of old Fort Hall. A troop of Oregon infantry composed of forty-four men was sent to Camp Lander in charge of Captain E. Palmer, First Oregon infantry volunteers. The post was abandoned in may 1866. Camp Halleck, which had been established in Idaho territory in 1862 was also abandoned in 1866.[215]

The government established a fort at Boise City, july 1863, in order to control the Snake Indians who

[214] U.S. Military order, St. Louis, headquarters, department of Missouri, august 2, october 23, 1866, MS. (Archives of Fort Meyer, Va.).

[215] Post history, Camp Lander, Idaho territory, MS. (War department, old records division, Washington, D.C.); Post returns, Camp Wallace, Idaho territory, september 20, 1865, MS. (War department, old records division, Washington, D.C.); Brown, Fort Hall, 336.

lived in that vicinity. Stone quarters for two hundred men were built, and frame stables for ten companies of cavalry. Camp Lyon was established in june 1865 on the north fork of Jordan creek, the northernmost tributary of the Owyhee river. Companies A, B, and D of the First Oregon infantry left Fort Boise june 19, 1865, and located Camp Lyon eight days later.[216]

The policy against the Indians of Idaho territory in 1864 was actively carried out by the government. Two companies of troops left Fort Boise on july 20 for the purpose of dispelling hostile Indians near Ruby City and Boonville on Jordan creek in the Owyhee region. The troops returned to the post on august 17, but no report of their activity has been recorded. Eleven days later Lieutenant Charles Hobart left Fort Boise with troops. Nineteen Indians were killed on the expedition and several camps were destroyed without loss of soldiers. Another troop left the fort january 31, 1865, under Captain Daniel O'Regan and returned march 12. During the campaign there was a skirmish along the Bruno river in which forty-two Indians were killed, seven captured, and four head of cattle taken. Lieutenant Charles West left the post may 12 with fifteen men of Company I, Washington territory, to chastise hostile Indians reported to be committing depredations on the overland route near Salmon Falls. On their return june 9 they said that no Indians had been seen and

---

216 Post returns, Camp Lyon, Idaho territory, june 1865, MS. (War department, old records division, Washington, D.C.) ; U.S. Medical histories of posts, MS. (War department, old records division, Washington, D.C.); U.S. Military stations and posts, 1872, 97, MS. (Archives of Fort Meyer, Va.).

that the trouble on the stage line had been caused by white men.[217]

In the spring of 1865, Fort Boise was called upon for aid against the Indians of Utah territory. On april 16, 1865, Paul Colvin, assistant superintendent of the Holladay line, wrote to Colonel O. H. Irish, superintendent of Indian affairs in Utah territory, saying that Indians were regularly attacking the line. The enemy claimed to be subjects of Pocatello, Indian chief of the Utah district. Colvin wrote as follows:

They have stolen several head of our mail stock, stripping the line completely of the stock at one time between Snake River station and Salmon Falls ferry. They have fired upon our employees and have driven others out of our stations. . .

Colvin accused the Indians of stealing provisions from stations and of threatening keepers at other times when food was not given them. He asked the aid of Colonel Irish in getting a military force to patrol the line, saying that the service must stop unless they were given such protection. In his reply Colonel Irish said that he had no military forces at his disposal and asked Colvin to call for aid at Fort Boise.[218]

In june Lieutenant James Curry, First Oregon infantry, took Company E, First Oregon cavalry, and twenty enlisted men of Company B, First Oregon infantry, from Fort Boise to establish Camp Reed at

[217] Post returns, Fort Boise, july, august, september, 1864, march, may, june, 1865, MS. (War department, old records division, Washington, D.C.).

[218] U.S. Department of interior, office of Indian affairs, commissioner's *report*, Utah territory, 1865.

Rock creek on the overland stage line. Captain Palmer took forty men of Company B to build another camp, eighty-five miles southeast of Fort Boise at Camas Prairie. This was to be called Camp Wallace and twenty-six soldiers were placed there. Thirty men of Companies G and I, Washington territory infantry, were ordered to leave the fort and to proceed to the "Farewell Bend" region of the Snake river in order to protect travelers and residents in that vicinity.

In the same month, Camp Lyon was built by soldiers from Fort Boise. On july 9 a detachment of the First Oregon cavalry from Fort Boise under Lieutenant Hobart engaged some Indians who had stolen livestock on Runnels creek. The soldiers surprised the camp and killed four Indians, wounded several others, and captured fifteen horses. On july 17, twenty-five soldiers of Companies A, B, and D from Camp Lyon made a surprise attack and killed four Indians in a camp on Jordan creek. They took an ox, two horses, and two revolvers, and destroyed dried meat, berries, robes, and blankets. Two privates were wounded.

Four hundred and five soldiers were stationed at Fort Boise in august under Lieutenant John Drake, First Oregon infantry. Some of these men performed service at Camp Lyon, Camp Reed, Forts Colvier and Walla Walla, Washington territory, and Camp Wallace. The commander of Camp Reed left with his troops august 18 to scout the headwaters of the Salmon and Rock creeks. On the three hundred mile trip the soldiers killed three Indians and captured three, destroyed six fisheries, and drove the tribe into the mountains.[219]

Indians living south of Fort Boise continued on the warpath during the fall of 1865. In october Captain James Powell's troops engaged them in battle sixty miles south of the fort and routed them without loss of soldiers.

That the tribes of Idaho territory resented the white invasion was clearly shown at a council in 1866 at which Governor Caleb Lyon, superintendent of Indian affairs of Idaho territory, made a treaty with the Shoshones. The Shoshone chief, Teho-nour-ha-ka, or Biting Bear, spoke eloquently as follows:

FATHER: I was born on this river; the bones of my fathers lie in the crevices of the rocks of these canyons, or in the springs of the valley. I want to stay here. Our wiki-ups are of straw; our arrowheads are stone; skins are our clothes; deer, elk, fish, antelope, roots and seed are our food. . . We desire to live here where we were born and to die here.

Biting Bear said that the Great Spirit had given the lands to the Indians and he asked the great father at Washington to take care of bad white and bad red men. In conclusion he said:

This day's words we will keep summer and winter, and we will punish all who break them. I am glad the war chief came with you. I see him with my eyes. Tell the great father at Washington you know my heart.

The desire for peace was strong in the hearts of many Indians of Idaho territory, yet in march 1866 sixteen peaceable Indian men, women, and children

---

[219] Post returns, Fort Boise, june, july, august, 1865, MS. (War department, old records division, Washington, D.C.).

were killed by white men fifteen miles above Idaho
City. Governor Lyon at once sent troops to protect
the rest of the tribe. In his report to the tribe's commissioner of Indian affairs he said, "In no case I have
examined have I found Indians the aggressor – always bad white men."

General Sherman, in a further effort to curb the
hostilities, issued an order in april to place Montana
territory and all routes leading to it in a separate
military department. General P. St. George Cooke
was appointed commander of the new department,
and troops were sent out after warring braves.[220] A
troop from Company M, First cavalry left Camp
Lyons on july 13 for a campaign which lasted until
october. The march covered seven hundred and
ninety-five miles, but only fifteen Indians were killed
during that time. A party of warring braves had surrounded thirty of the soldiers on september 28 and
compelled them to retreat from the region. Later, on
october 31, detachment E of the Twenty-third infantry
attacked a camp of Snake Indians on Owyhee river
and killed five warriors. Several Indians were
wounded, eight captured, thirty-eight horses taken,
as well as two mules and an ox; the camp was destroyed and a large supply of ammunition and provisions was ruined.[221]

Indians in Montana territory caused little damage

220 San Francisco *daily evening bulletin,* may 14, june 14, 1866; Atchison (Kans.) *daily free press,* june 1, 1866; Camp Douglas (Utah terr.)
daily union vedette, october 4, 1865.

221 U.S. Muster rolls, october 1866, MS. (War department, old records
division, Washington, D.C.).

to the Holladay property. The stage line, located in the extreme western part of the territory, did not cross much valuable hunting ground. The Snake and Bannock tribes of this section were generally at peace with the whites during 1865 and 1866. By 1866 they were in a terrible condition and badly in need of aid, lacking even the bare necessities of life. Governor Thomas F. Meagher called them a "revolting reproach to our civilization." The hostile Blackfeet were located east of Virginia City. Their raids on the route between Virginia City and Helena City in 1866 caused Governor Meagher to request the founding of military posts with permanent garrisons. Fort Benton was located about one hundred miles northeast of Helena City. In Meagher's opinion more forts were needed in such a large territory. Nevertheless, conditions were not bad enough to require a large amount of equipment for the maintenance of the tri-weekly schedule on the routes between Salt Lake City, Boise City, and Virginia City.[222]

Holladay had been much less fortunate on his main line. In 1880 the congressional committee on claims received the sworn testimony of twenty-four Holladay employees and United States officers in regard to his losses from Indian depredations and at the hands of the soldiers. The testimonies differed with reference to location and time of occurrence. Affidavits of losses, not including two removals of the stage route, varied in amount from $300 to $134,958;

[222] U.S. Department of interior, office of Indian affairs, commissioner's *report*, Montana, 1866.

the total amount of damages claimed was $390,067.60. The committee on claims reported Holladay's total losses to be as follows:

Indian depredations	$369,739
Removal of line, 1862	$ 77,000
Removal of line, 1864	$ 50,000
Property taken by soldiers	$ 30,000

Grand Total $526,739 [223]

Although the maintenance of the important overland stage line in time of crisis had resulted in the loss of a fortune to Holladay, he was accused of charging for the transportation of his coach escorts. In august 1865 Alexander Bliss, quartermaster-general, had advised Colonel J. A. Potter, chief quartermaster at Fort Leavenworth, that the rates on stage routes west of the Missouri should be changed in such a way that those lines which had military escorts should charge regular passenger rates and rates for extra baggage, less thirty-three and one-third per cent. It was stipulated that lines which used no escort

[223] U.S. Senate. *Miscellaneous documents,* 46 cong., 2 sess., I, no. 19, 64; *Report,* 46 cong., 2 sess., I, no. 216, 9. The different affidavits were:

A. L. Pease and others	$41,400.00	Seaman Johnson, *et al.*	$ 300.00
J. A. Slade, *et al.*	12,150.00	James Stewart, *et al.*	16,310.00
S. B. Babcock, *et al.*	8,310.00	R. J. Spotswood, *et al.*	14,550.00
J. E. Bromley, *et al.*	7,448.00	George H. Carlyle,	
William A. Reid, *et al.*	5,200.00	Solomon Riddle, *et al.*	49,086.00
George M. Lloyd, Charles Irwins, S. O. Jerome, *et al.*			15,008.00
Reuben S. Thomas, William Reynolds, *et al.*			59,217.60
Captain E. B. Murphy, U.S. army, *et al.*			7,200.00

William Hudnut, Richard Quinn, R. S. Thomas, A. S. Hughes, Solomon Riddle, Lieutenant Brewer, U.S. army, *et al.* (burning of Julesburg, Colorado territory) 134,958.00

Lem Flowers, Richard Murray, William A. Trotter, *et al.* 18,930.00

Grand total $390,067.60

could charge regular rates providing the charge did not exceed ten cents a mile. In 1867 Secretary Stanton ordered the quartermaster-general to pay the thirty-three and one-third per cent which had been withheld, since the officers of the quartermaster department had arranged for no such stipulation with Holladay.[224]

During the time of Indian wars in the west the Civil war had taken the spotlight and western affairs had been almost excluded from the news. It was only after the boom of cannon and the rush of arrows had ceased that any estimate could be made of the handling of the Indian problem. The Indians had been greatly abused by the white man in general. After the United States government had adopted the reservation and annuity policy, traders had stolen annuities from the Indians. Miners had crossed their reservations and driven away the game which gave food and shelter to the red people. Buffalo were ruthlessly slaughtered and left to rot on the prairies. Border gunmen had taken almost the same attitude toward the Indians that hunters had taken toward the buffalo; they killed them without cause, for sport. Occurrences of this kind had sent the tribes on the warpath, partly to protect their families, partly to secure better treaties with the government so that they might enrich their store of money, sugar, blankets, and other needful things. The government was not always wise in handling its problem, but it was greatly taxed at the time with a more serious one. Nevertheless, the

[224] Quartermaster-general's book, august 2, 1865, september 30, 1867, MS. (Archives of Fort Meyer, Va.).

general verdict was that its Indian policy between 1861 and 1866 had been a failure.

Holladay, too, had received his share of criticism, but he had never been ridiculed, as had the United States army. The Indian had great respect for the stagecoaches, which they called "fire-boxes" at the time of military escort. They had even greater respect for the Holladay horses, coveting them as speedier than the government mounts. The stagecoach, to the Indian, was the symbol of a civilization which was to wipe out the red man. Their anger was toward the symbol, not toward the Holladay line.[225]

After the trouble with the Indian was over, or at least well in hand because of sufficient military protection, Holladay presented his claim for losses to congress. The claim was presented in january 1866 and there were favorable reports concerning it, but congress passed no appropriation for his benefit. On march 26, 1866, in the thirty-ninth congress, a joint resolution was passed in the house of representatives to refer Holladay's case to the court of claims. On may 12 the house joint resolution was taken up in the senate, amended, and passed. The house refused to concur and both houses appointed conference committees, but congress adjourned without taking final action.

Holladay was never, in fact, paid for the great service he had given his country. The matter was postponed, and finally, in 1877 congress offered one hundred thousand dollars to settle the account. This was less than one-fifth of the claim. It is character-

225 *Army and navy journal,* III, 653.

istic of the impetuous westerner that he refused the amount, saying that if the United States was not able to pay its debts he would give it his claim. He is said to have left Washington immediately and never to have returned.

Though Holladay absented himself from Washington, the matter of his claims against the government dragged on for more than thirty years. In 1878 Senator Angus Cameron, a member of the committee on claims, again reported to the senate that the amount due Holladay was $526,739; ten years later, on april 23, 1888, a bill was proposed to pay Mrs. Holladay $320,153 for the losses, but failed to pass. In 1901 Holladay's heirs sued for the full amount of $526,739. While this case was still in the court, another bill was introduced in the senate, january 21, 1907, for an appropriation of $526,739 to pay for Holladay's losses and expenses in changing the mail route. This bill was read twice and referred to the committee on claims, but did not pass. Finally the claim of Holladay's heirs was overruled by the court of claims on november 18, 1912, and the case was dismissed.[226]

---

[226] U.S. House. *Report,* 47 cong., 1 sess., IV, no. 1182, 1; Ben Holladay vs. United States, 1-4, MS. (Court of claims, Washington, D.C.).

Holladay Abdicates

Holladay Abdicates

The picture that confronted Holladay in 1866 would have discouraged any but the stoutest heart. His losses of property during the Indian wars of 1864 and 1865 had been severe, and in addition to these losses his business was endangered by competition on the central route. Nevertheless, he was determined to continue his operations and to crush his rivals.

The rivalry of the two young Kansas towns, Atchison and Leavenworth, had fostered the rivalry of the two stage lines, the Holladay company and the Butterfield Overland Despatch line. Atchison had attracted the southern sympathizers as settlers, while Leavenworth was settled mainly by those from the free states. Leavenworth was not content that Atchison should control one end of the lucrative stage line between the Missouri river and Denver. In an effort to overcome the Holladay monopoly the city was instrumental in starting a new stage line over the Smoky Hill route. And thus was encouraged a further rivalry – between the Platte river and the Smoky Hill routes – which had existed since the days of Russell, Majors, and Waddell.

In the fall of 1864, Dave Butterfield, formerly of Denver, who had moved to Atchison in the summer to start a commission business, had conceived the plan of running a freight line between Atchison and Denver by way of the Smoky Hill river valley in Kansas. He proceeded to establish an office in New York City and soon secured the backing of an eastern company with assets of six million dollars cash. The Butterfield Overland Despatch line, which became popularly known as the B.O.D. was organized in the spring of 1865. The route chosen for the freight line was about sixty-one miles shorter than the Holladay line, but as it lacked military protection it was also more hazardous. Consequently when the city of Leavenworth approached Butterfield for aid in opening a new stage route to Denver he accepted the offer with the provision that protection be given the new line. Leavenworth staged a drive for funds, and with the approval of the acting mayor, C. N. Palmer, promised to pay the B.O.D. four thousand dollars upon completion of the line. The city's interest in fostering a line which started from Atchison lay in its plan to have wagon and stagecoach connections with the rival town. It was also expected that the new route would bring Leavenworth increased trade from the west.

Butterfield's first wagons, loaded with machinery and other freight, were hauled out of Atchison by ox- and mule-teams in the summer of 1865. So successful was his freighting business that Butterfield was encouraged to promise stagecoach service within sixty days. The city of Leavenworth eagerly awaited the opening of the new schedule, which it was anticipated would be faster than that of the Holladay line. However, Butterfield was handicapped by delays in road building and in organization of the system, and the sixty-day promise was not kept.[227] Arrangements had been made with the Adams, American, and United States Express companies to carry express in the coaches. Although there was still no definite guarantee of military protection the B.O.D. line began operation in september, and on september 23 the first Overland Despatch coach rolled into Denver.

Dave Butterfield was a passenger on the first coach, and his former town awaited his arrival with enthusiasm. He had many friends among the miners, merchants, and contractors. The Denver delegates had prepared a great celebration. Leading citizens, accompanied by the First Colorado band, rode four miles eastward from the city to await the coming of the dashing, rolling Concord coach. Dave Butterfield stepped from the stage to greet the delegation with enthusiasm. Flags waved, the band played, and flowery speeches were made. Banners blazoned forth such messages as "Welcome Dave and Your Express" and "Westward the course of Empire takes its way." In the words of those times, it was a gala occasion. Upon their arrival in Denver there was a street celebration, and a banquet at the Planters hotel ended the events of a glorious day.[228]

The B.O.D. line had high hopes of success. Twenty good stages were bought in Chicago. Express-coaches were run tri-weekly between Atchison, Leavenworth, and Denver and an eight-day schedule was main-

[227] *Rocky mountain news* (Denver), may 24, 1866. D. A. Butterfield should not be confused with John Butterfield on the southern mail route 1858-1861.

[228] *Rocky mountain news* (Denver), september 27, 1865; Smiley, *History of Denver*, 364.

tained. The firm planned to run a daily stage between Denver and Santa Fe after october 1, 1865, and also a tri-weekly stage line between Denver and Salt Lake City which would carry merchandise at express rates. Agents were placed at New York, Boston, Philadelphia, Chicago, St. Louis, Leavenworth, Lawrence, Denver, and Salt Lake City. Butterfield himself was general superintendent and manager of the line.

The new road to the west attracted its share of thrill seekers. Several Indian tribes whose hunting grounds were crossed by the stage line had announced their intention of stopping this new invasion by the palefaces. Butterfield had fully realized these dangers and had bought tough fast mules to pull his Concord coaches across the western plains. Passengers on the early trips of the B.O.D. line went well protected by Ballard rifles, navy revolvers, and strong sheath knives. Even with this wealth of equipment, few could watch the moving prairie for signs of danger with any degree of calmness.

One passenger on the new line, writing of his travels, said that the stage had left Atchison on a november morning in 1865 and reached St. Mary's mission on the Potawatomi reservation about seventy miles away by nightfall. The passengers remained in the coach that night but spent little time in sleep, entertaining themselves with lively stories and in singing songs. On the second day, he said, the stage traveled through a rolling country covered with high grass. Many black-tailed deer were seen and buffalos galloped lazily away from the road when the stage neared them. Fort Ellsworth was reached the follow-

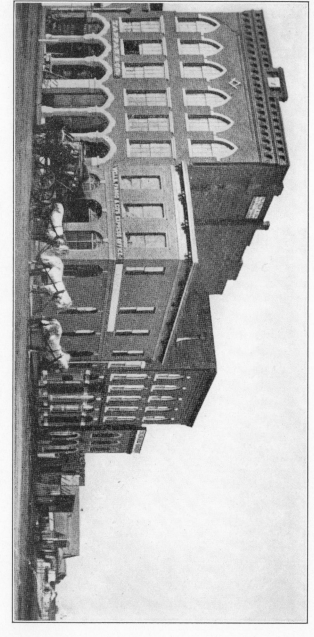

CORNER OF FIFTEENTH AND MARKET STREETS, DENVER, 1868

ing night, and the weary travelers unloaded to look for food. Their appetites, sharp by this time, were satisfied with a meal of venison, baked potatoes, corn dodgers, and coffee. The party spent fifteen days on the trip, reaching Denver on december 2 without having experienced any trouble from Indians.

Home stations on the Butterfield line, usually a one-story frame house with stable and sheds, were about forty miles apart. Butterfield in his attempt to better Holladay's time between Denver and eastern Kansas arranged to keep fresh animals to haul the stagecoaches, replacing them at points about fifteen miles apart. Drivers were changed at the home stations.[229]

In january 1866 the Butterfield company secured a thirty-year charter from the Kansas legislature. Edward P. Bray, William R. Brewster, W. A. Loveland, T. H. Messenger, C. G. Hammond, and D. A. Butterfield were its backers. In the charter the firm was given the right to build and use a wagon road from Denver up Cherry creek, Beaver creek, Corn creek, Eureka creek, and past Cheyenne Wells to the eastern boundary of Colorado territory. Permission was given to build a stage line to Santa Fe and also to build a branch to the western boundary of Colorado territory by way of one of the few passes then known through the mountains. The company owned the right of way for three miles along both sides of the route, had mining rights to any lodes discovered on its property, was privileged to dig wells

[229] *Daily Kansas state journal* (Lawrence), october 6, 1865; *Harper's new monthly magazine*, CCVI, 137-145, 150.

and ditches, and also to build bridges and inclosures. Permission was also given in the charter to build a telegraph line with necessary stations and offices along the company's route. The grant to carry express was valuable, as a large amount of gold and other ore was being sent eastward from the territory and quantities of merchandise were shipped westward to mining camps in the Rockies. Private parties, according to the charter, should be permitted use of the road and railroad charters over the road could be granted. At this time the Kansas Pacific had been built from Kansas City, or Wyandotte, to Lawrence, and was expected to build farther westward in 1866.[230]

The receipt of the liberal charter was no guarantee, however, against troubles on the B.O.D. line. Lack of sufficient military protection had permitted Indian depredations during the fall and winter of 1865, with consequent financial loss. The company was also unable to build a telegraph line from Denver to Central City. Its hope for extension westward from Denver lay in the promise of Wells, Fargo and company to build a stage line from Salt Lake City by way of the Berthoud pass. This plan also was to be thwarted, though at the time the plan had been formulated there was every reason to expect the building of such a line. Wells, Fargo and company had built up a great express business in the far west during the gold rush days, and had expanded to carry express between California and Salt Lake City by means of a regular

---

[230] Colorado territory legislative *laws*, 1866, 113-115; Smiley, *History of Denver*, 304. Other backers were W. H. Fogg, T. R. Davis, George E. Cook, J. H. Frileston of New York, Charles F. Holly, W. H. Gale, G. A. Hinsdale, C. A. Cook, Frank Hall, and B. R. Colvin of Colorado territory.

stage line. The firm had also attempted to carry express on Holladay's line between Colorado territory and Utah territory, but had been unable to come to terms with Holladay. They had been backed, in their fight to make Holladay accede to their wishes, by the American Express company and the United States Express company. After their failure to move Holladay the proverbial inch they had unwisely announced that they would build a competing line to Denver and fight him for his profitable business. It was with this proposed line that the Butterfield company hoped to connect at Denver.

Holladay saw what it would mean to his own business to have a competing line with a through route from the Missouri to the Pacific. As usual, he rose to the emergency. He at once sent out two of his inspectors to check over the B.O.D. line with respect to the number of its employees, their work, and the details of all equipment and schedules. When the full report was received, Holladay learned something which spurred him to immediate action. The Butterfield firm was operating under very heavy expenses and was in fact almost bankrupt.

One evening in march 1866, at a secluded table in Delmonico's restaurant in New York City, Holladay and Edward P. Bray had a quiet talk. The imperious Holladay, gazing fixedly at the short elderly president of the B.O.D., told him that the line had already lost more than a million dollars and that they must sell at Holladay's price or look forward to certain ruin. Bray realized he had no choice and finally, and reluctantly, agreed to sell to Holladay. So the B.O.D line, after operating for about a year and a half, went out of existence and Holladay, his last competitor defeated, was stagecoach king indeed. He uttered a final defiant challenge to the express companies in return for their threat to build a rival line. "Answer those express companies," he told his secretary, "and tell them to stock and be d—d!" He was confident that now, with all hope gone of connecting with the B.O.D. line at Denver, they would make no further attempt to build a stage line.

The charter, route, and all equipment of the Butterfield company were included in the purchase. Holladay undoubtedly knew at the time of the purchase that the railroads were encroaching on the route. The Union Pacific railroad was building through Nebraska territory and the Kansas Pacific was extending toward the central part of Kansas. A man of his financial astuteness would not have purchased the stage line at this time had he not believed it to be a safe investment. He knew, also, that the railroad would eventually displace the stagecoach, but he expected the latter to be used as an auxiliary at the ends of the lines, and he thought the railroad's advance would be slow.[231]

Before 1866 progress on the railroads had been slow indeed, a condition for which Holladay believed the Civil war to be responsible. As late as april 1866 the Holladay Overland Mail and Express company was running its coaches on regular schedule from

---

[231] Banning and Banning, *Six horses,* 343, 344; Harlow, *Old waybills,* 252; Junction City (Kans.) *union,* april 7, 1866; Atchison (Kans.) *daily free press,* march 17, 1866.

Omaha to the west. The building of the railroad seemed to be progressing at no more than a snail's pace across the plains. Holladay, knowing what the railroad company faced when the outposts of civilization were reached – the lack of timber and the hostility of Indian tribes – expected it to continue at the same pace. But instead construction began to advance so rapidly that by july 4 the road was completed for service to Columbus, Nebraska territory. On august 16 it had extended to Lone Tree station, only sixty-five miles east of Fort Kearny, and on august 20 it reached the fort. Workmen, their rifles near at hand for protection against Indians, were pushing the line westward to meet the Central Pacific which was building from California.[232]

As the Union Pacific advanced, the stagecoach lines began to decline. On july 30 the postmaster-general ordered Holladay to curtail service on route no. 14260 (Atchison to Salt Lake City). Mail was henceforth to be delivered only three times a week between Atchison and Guittard's station in Kansas and only once a week to Big Sandy. Service between Big Sandy and Fort Kearny was to be discontinued. Transportation, however, was to commence between Denver and the ends of the division in Nebraska territory and Kansas. Holladay was ordered to make two separate lines of service between Denver and the ends of the divisions and to continue a daily service between Denver and

---

[232] *Ibid.,* march 24, 1866; Omaha *weekly herald,* march 30, 1866; Leavenworth (Kans.) *daily conservative,* august 27, 1866; Black Hawk (Colo. terr.) *mining journal,* august 1, 1866; *Rocky mountain news* (Denver) july 4, 1866.

Salt Lake City. Although at this time his old rate of pay as mail contractor was supposed to continue with the new service, in the fall Postmaster-general Alex W. Randall announced that it would be reduced pro rata as the railroad from Omaha extended toward Denver.[233]

The Kansas Pacific also had invaded the Holladay territory, although it was at that time known as the Union Pacific railroad, eastern division. It had been organized in 1863 under the railroad act which had been passed by congress in 1862, and had secured control of the Leavenworth, Pawnee, and Western railroad during the summer of 1864. The latter company had started construction of a line westward from Leavenworth. Trouble with the building contractors had delayed the construction of the road. Difficulties with city officials in Leavenworth over costs of supplies and payment of money guarantees soon followed and the owners of the railroad, George Fremont and Samuel Hallett, changed the eastern terminus from Leavenworth to Wyandotte, Kansas. The disturbance culminated in the murder of Hallett by O. A. Talcott, chief engineer of the railroad. Under the direction of Superintendent E. M. Bartholomew, construction of the line was pushed and it reached Lawrence on november 26, 1864. Regular service was established to Topeka on january 1, 1866. By march 2 of that year the construction had reached Silver Lake and plans were made to extend the road rapidly to Manhattan.

However, the company made an important change

---

[233] U.S. House. *Executive documents,* 40 cong., 2 sess., XV, no. 201, exhibit B, 2.

in its route before that city was reached. The original charter had granted the right to construct a railroad up the Republican river valley which would connect with the Union Pacific in Nebraska territory. The citizens of Colorado territory, especially in Denver, had been discouraged when they learned the Union Pacific in Nebraska territory would not build to their city. They persuaded the railroad company then building in Kansas to change its route in order that Denver might have a railroad connection. On july 3, 1866, congress authorized the Union Pacific, eastern division, to select its general route and join the Union Pacific at a point not over fifty miles west of a meridian passing through Denver. As the Union Pacific, eastern division had realized that it could not construct its line to the one hundredth meridian in Nebraska territory before the Union Pacific reached that point, it was glad to receive permission to change the route. The new way selected was to extend westward from Salina up the Smoky Hill river valley.

The railroad construction was hastened toward Manhattan. By july 2 passenger trains were going as far as St. Marys, twenty-six miles west of Topeka, and by august 18 they had reached Manhattan. Railroad tracks had been laid one-half mile beyond the city. This rapid pace was necessarily shortening the stagecoach transportation routes. On august 15 the postmaster-general ordered Holladay to carry mail in his coaches between Manhattan and Denver. The stage company was at that time carrying through mail from Denver on tuesday, thursday, and saturday mornings on the Smoky Hill route for St. Joseph,

St. Louis, and other eastern cities. Through mails were received at Denver by this route on the same mornings. On september 12 the schedule was increased to daily service and the time of departure from Denver was changed to four in the afternoon. Holladay's mail-coaches were running daily from Manhattan as late as september 15, 1866.[234]

On october 24 the Kansas Pacific company laid its first rails west of the Republican river at Junction City. A locomotive was running to the river by that time and a bridge was being rushed to completion. In the summer of that year Junction City had been a mere village consisting of six wooden shanties. The Holladay coaches stopped there while passengers ate a meal of hot cakes, tomatoes, and tea.

This trip was amusingly described in 1866 by William Dixon, an Englishman, going west from Junction City. He wrote that the Holladay Concord coach was replaced at this point by a light frame wagon which had no doors. Only the canvas roof and flapping canvas blinds served as protection, and these failed to keep off a driving rain which descended upon them. On climbing into the wagon at Junction City the passengers found it already full of mail-sacks, but they were told optimistically that the rough roads would soon cause the mail-bags to shake down so that there would be more room. This prediction proved to be true, but the inadequate wagon springs increased the discomfort and unpleasantness of the

234 *Kansas radical* (Manhattan), august 18, september 15, 1866; *Rocky mountain news* (Denver), september 8, 12, 1866; Atchison (Kans.) *daily free press,* june 29, 1866; Postmaster-general's *report,* 1866 in U.S. House. *Executive documents,* 39 cong., 2 sess., IV, no. 1.

ride. Crowded conditions were hardly improved by the varied assortment of luggage, pistols, maps, potted meats, cigar cases, umbrellas, and many a flask of brandy. No military escort accompanied the wagon at this time, although it carried the United States mail, and few soldiers were seen in the region.

Dixon had boarded the coach at Wamego, having paid five hundred dollars for a ticket to Salt Lake City. The mules, he said, were changed every forty to fifty miles. The wagon jogged steadily westward with its passengers and mail. Hot tired eyes were soothed by the green of shady groves along the river, which was never far from the trail. When a mail-bag was shaken from the wagon and fell to the ground, the mules were slowly circled over the grass-matted prairie to retrieve the lost bag, and gay prairie flowers were trampled until the wagon was again in the deep rutted roadway leading toward the mountains. Great herds of buffalo, elk, antelope, and black-tailed deer watched the stage from a safe distance. During forty hours of the westward journey Dixon saw them, and they seemed to be countless. Other wild game was plentiful; even prairie dogs, when well cooked, were considered enjoyable food in this region.

Riding in their miserable den the travelers were oppressed by rain, sand, and dust. They were banged, beaten, and jolted, their heads were swollen and their faces bruised. Heads ached, nostrils were choked with sand, limbs were stiffened and bent with cramps. Sometimes the disheartened travelers would leave the stage to rinse their mouths and dip their heads in some little creek, the water of which they did not dare to drink. Then, walking several miles ahead of the stage, they felt like new men again and forgot the discomforts of their ride in the brisk morning air while they looked on the beautiful prairie scenery. After such experiences, it can well be imagined that the coming of the railroad, with its easy, comparatively safe travel, was welcomed by every western traveler.[235]

The completion of the Union Pacific to Fort Kearny from Omaha decreased Holladay's stage business between Atchison and Fort Kearny. Many travelers from the east now arranged their trips to the west by way of Omaha instead of through northeastern Kansas. The eastern mail also was sent from Fort Kearny to Omaha by railroad. Holladay, therefore, needed fewer coaches on his Atchison–Fort Kearny division. In august he sent twenty-five overland coaches from Atchison to Manhattan on the Smoky Hill route to furnish transportation between Denver and the western end of the railroad. The last coaches from Holladay's Kearny division passed through Marysville august 25 on their way to Junction City, twenty miles from Manhattan.

In Nebraska territory freight and passenger trains were going daily between Omaha and Fort Kearny, while Holladay had his Denver–Salt Lake City coaches furnishing daily service from the Fort Kearny terminal to western cities. The coaches were scheduled to run from Denver to Fort Kearny in two days twenty-two hours, and to arrive at the fort at six

---

[235] Junction City (Kans.) *union,* october 27, 1866; Dixon, *New America,* I, 25, 37, 38, 48, 91, 93, 130.

each evening. The fare was one hundred and fifty dollars between Fort Kearny and Denver, and three hundred dollars between Fort Kearny and Salt Lake City.[236]

The first passenger train entered Junction City on november 10, and two days later a regular schedule was commenced. By november 27 the Kansas Pacific railroad was completed to Chapman's creek, about eight miles above Junction City. As the railroad moved westward and established a car schedule, the stage line was shortened. On november 27 the stage fare was reduced to one hundred dollars from Denver to Atchison by way of the Platte and Smoky Hill routes, and the express rate was announced as thirty-five cents a pound.

In august Holladay controlled the following lines:

Topeka to Denver, Smoky Hill route	585 miles
Atchison to Denver, Platte route	650 miles
Omaha to Fort Kearny	150 miles
Denver to Salt Lake City	600 miles
Salt Lake City to Montana mines with branches (about)	600 miles
Junction on Montana line to Boise City, Idaho territory	370 miles
Local lines from Denver	40 miles
Nebraska City to Fort Kearny	150 miles
Grand Total	3145 miles

Holladay, secure on his throne as stagecoach king, nevertheless saw that the golden era of his business

[236] Rusling, *Great west*, 41, 207; Black Hawk (Colo. terr.) *mining journal*, august 1, 1866; Leavenworth (Kans.) *daily conservative*, august 27, 30, 1866.

was almost at an end. He preferred abdication to dethronement. If someone not as far-seeing coveted his crown, he was willing to sell his extensive stage business to the highest bidder.[237]

In 1865 Louis McLane, president of the Overland Mail company in which Wells, Fargo and company were heavy investors, had journeyed over the Holladay lines. It was rumored at the time that he planned to buy the eastern part of the overland line between Atchison and California. Holladay had no desire to sell in 1865, and in 1866 he checkmated McLane's plans for uniting the Overland Mail line with the Butterfield Overland Despatch route by buying out Butterfield. However, so quickly had come the changes in the stagecoach business that by october of the same year he was ready to sell.

On november 1 the sale took place, and the corporate name of the Holladay Overland Mail and Express company was changed on december 10 to Wells, Fargo and company. The new officers of the consolidated company were Louis McLane, president; George K. Otis, secretary; and Calvin Goddard, treasurer. The price received for the sale of his stage company was vastly different from the amount Holladay had paid for the Central Overland California and Pike's Peak company in 1862. According to the terms of the sale he received one million five hundred thousand dollars in cash, three hundred thousand dollars worth of stock in Wells, Fargo and company, and

237 Junction City (Kans.) *union*, november 17, 1866; *Rocky mountain news* (Denver), november 27, 1866; Banning and Banning, *Six horses*, 343-345.

became a director of the new firm. A short time later he sold his stock to raise funds for another business venture.[238]

Six months after the sale Holladay saw his prophecy of a quick decline come true. He had been fortunate that Wells, Fargo and company had disagreed with him. Its directors believed that the stagecoach would be the important means of transportation between Salt Lake City and Nebraska territory, as well as between Salt Lake City and Colorado territory, for at least six years longer. They had been most eager to buy. Holladay had been wise in leaving the field while there was a demand for his equipment. In 1869, when the Union Pacific and Central Pacific railroads were completed in Utah territory to make a continuous rail route between Omaha and Sacramento, he would have received much less for his property. As it was, he retired a victor.

The abdicating stagecoach king must have felt truly satisfied as he looked back over the years of his service. At times he had been ruthless, but it was a part of his creed that the end justified the means. He had developed and owned the best-equipped stage line in the west. He had kept, as nearly as was possible at the time, to a high standard of regular schedules, disciplined employees, and excellent service. He had lost a quarter of a million dollars through the Indian wars and yet had possessed the courage to expand his

[238] Atchison (Kans.) *daily free press,* november 2, 1866; Central City (Colo. terr.) *daily miner's register,* november 4, 13, 1866; Omaha *weekly republican,* november 9, 1866; Smiley, *History of Denver,* 363; Rusling, *Great West,* 207.

business. The railroad sealed the fate of the Indians who fought to prevent transportation across the plains even as it wrote finish to the days of prosperity for the stagecoach business. The courageous Holladay was ready to retire and glad to see the stagecoach superseded by a better means of transportation.

Holladay the Man

Holladay the Man

Back somewhere in Scotch history there had been a Sir William Holladay, but as a boy Ben Holladay had known only the humble environment of a Kentucky farm, where his parents had given him an example of hard work and frugal living. He was one of seven children, six boys and a girl, all of whom were for a time residents of Weston, Missouri. Joseph Holladay, who remained a bachelor, was later associated with his famous brother in the stagecoach business at Salt Lake City. Jesse was an early pioneer to California and afterward became interested in the real estate business in Chicago. Andrew practised medicine at Nebraska City, Nebraska. James H. Holladay, who was of assistance to Ben during the early days of his stagecoach business, moved to Colorado territory from Weston. His wife died there and he returned with his small daughter in 1873. The only sister, Frances, married a man named Downey and remained in Weston until her death.[239]

David Holladay, usually called Dave, was Ben's favorite brother. Both were sandy haired in their youth and looked somewhat alike. Ben aided Dave in starting several business enterprises. The packing

239 *Catholic tribune* (St. Joseph, Mo.), june 1, 22, 1895; Holladay, Hattie, interview with author, 1, 2, MS.; Root and Connelley, *Overland stage*, 452.

plant near Weston, which they owned together, Dave later turned into a flour mill, and in 1856 into the Blue Springs distillery which made excellent Bourbon whisky. For a few years the brothers lived across the road from one another in homes near Weston. Dave finally bought the Weston home of Theodore Warner, Ben's freighting partner.

Of the seven Holladays, Ben alone became nationally and internationally famous. He was far more than the manager of a stagecoach company. First of all he was a dynamic and colorful personality. And he was a sensationally successful financier. In addition to his stagecoach line, he made successful ventures into the steamship business and the mining industry. The Ophir Silver mine, in Nevada territory, was the source of a minor fortune, and in the east where he owned a magnificent estate called Ophir Place, he was known as "the silver king."

Holladay's fondness for luxurious living quarters caused him to own several pretentious homes up to the time of his retirement from the stagecoach business. A friend once said that Ben wanted the halls of his Weston mansion big enough to drive a wagon through, and with this idea in mind all his homes must have been selected.

The Weston home had wide halls dividing the house upstairs and down. The largest front room downstairs was twenty by twenty-five feet, and across the hall was a room sixteen by twenty feet. Beautiful crystal chandeliers hung from the ceilings, and there were marble fireplaces in these two rooms as well as in the northwest bedroom upstairs. The house had

BEN HOLLADAY

sixteen rooms, nine upstairs, five below, and behind
the rear porch were two additional rooms used for
slave quarters. There was a spacious yard surrounded
by a four-foot stone wall. At the rear was a rambling
stable with room for twenty horses, and hitching-posts
stood near the front wall. The house stands today, a
relic of the time when hospitality was extended with
a generous flourish.

When Holladay became a mail contractor he found
it advisable to buy a home in Washington. Before he
could be paid for his contracts it was necessary to
have the approval of the president, members of congress, and the postal department, and the maintenance
of friendly relations was a matter of importance. The
Washington home was on K street, opposite Franklin
square. Through its bronze doors came many national
leaders and titled Europeans.[240] Holladay and his
attractive red-haired wife were genuinely hospitable,
and their receptions something more than empty
splendor. The former farm boy surrounded himself
with evidences of culture as well as with luxuries.
There was a large classical library and also many
other valuable books, oil paintings by great masters,
and fine tapestries. The marble floor, bronzes, and
marble statuary in the dining-room were formally
decorative. The bronze lions were reported to have
cost six thousand dollars each. A vault held the valuable Holladay jewels when they were not being worn
to dazzle Washington society.

Holladay also owned a brownstone mansion in New

---

[240] *Catholic tribune* (St. Joseph, Mo.), june 1, 22, 1895; Dawson scrap-
book (Library of Colorado state historical society), XIV, 131.

York City, in order to be near his business offices on Williams street. There, as well, he received social recognition, and became a member of the exclusive Union Club.

Of all his homes, Ophir Place in Westchester county, New York, was the most magnificent. It was a gem of a beautiful thousand acre tract at White Plains, about sixty miles from New York City. Its original cost was said to have been about one million dollars, while the landscaping was estimated to have cost ten thousand dollars. A buffalo herd fed in the park, and a narrow-gauge railroad ran to the place.[241]

Mrs. Holladay loved society, and society apparently loved coming to Ophir Place, for during certain months of the year the cost of entertainment alone was estimated at seven thousand dollars. However, with all the social recognition the Holladays were receiving, their families were not neglected. Into their home they took William and Clara, the small children of Dave Holladay, who attended a good school near-by and must have thought themselves transported to paradise.

Holladay's joy in Ophir Place came to an abrupt end. His wife died there. According to her wish she was buried in the family chapel near the mansion, with her favorite flowers growing outside. Eventually both home and chapel were lost. With Holladay's permission the chapel was torn down and his wife's body removed to Rye, New York. A fortune had been lost in a western railroad, and Ophir Place

---

241 Root and Connelley, *Overland stage,* 440, 441, 452; Baker, letter to author, 1, 2, MS.

one of them." He was often pleased to turn business deals to their profit. [246]

Not always so kindly with his enemies, he had a reputation for bluntness. Employees who displeased him were treated with sharp severity. Greatly burdened as he was with business worries, it is not surprising that he should be curt in his reproofs, and since he was generally courteous and kindly toward those who worked for him, the majority loved as well as respected him. They understood that business came first with him. He was irascible when crossed. Great lover of good horse-flesh as he was, he counted it for nothing when time must be considered and wore out many a fine steed on his record trips across the country.

The rushing speed of the life he forced himself to live soon told on his body. He was described in 1866 as of "indifferent health." On one of his hurried journeys across the country he took his physician with him, but he apparently had no time to be sick.

That he had time to cultivate friends and achieve popularity is remarkable in itself. He was popular partly because he loved a good joke. Once he ate copiously of some hot soup offered him by a friendly Indian. When he had finished the old chief said, "Well, Ben, how like soup?" Holladay answered, "Very well! What kind of soup is it?" The chief laughed and said, "Very fine dog soup!" Holladay often told the joke on himself. [247]

---

[246] *Catholic tribune* (St. Joseph, Mo.), june 22, 1895; Poss, interview with author, 1, 2, MS.

[247] *Ibid.;* Holladay, Hattie, interview with author, 1, 2, MS.; Dawson scrap-book (Library of Colorado state historical society), XIV, 115.

If he was at ease eating "dog soup" with the Indians he was equally at ease with society in the east. In fact he was popular all over the nation. Racehorses and cigars were named for him. A proof of his popularity came as early as 1862 when he figured in a disaster on the Pacific ocean. He was traveling on a Pacific coast steamer, the "Golden Gate," off the western coast of Mexico when a fire broke out. The fire separated passengers in the bow from those in the stern. The ship was headed for the breakers. After twenty-five minutes of anxiety Holladay left the boat by going down the forward chains. He was swept under the paddle wheel. Grabbing it, he was turned round and round until he became badly bruised and beaten. He was injured further by the rudder, but finally managed to seize a ladder on the side of the ship. Weak as he was, he had the dogged determination to hold on for two hours until a boat from the ship rescued him. The survivors managed to reach the shore after a two-hour battle with the strong current. The California newspaper telling of the disaster said, "The news of the safety of this gentleman relieved thousands of anxious hearts." [248]

Imposing in appearance, abounding in vitality and energy, his pleasant face partially hidden by a heavy black beard and mustache, his eyes alternately kind and sharp, he attracted attention wherever he went. His clothes were described as unique, and he was fond of wearing costly jewels. Yet these superficial characteristics might have won him only a cheap popularity had he not also been a truly great man.

[248] *Ibid.,* xiv, 131; San Francisco *daily evening bulletin,* august 7, 1862.

According to James Rusling, he was "of large grasp and quick perceptions." R. M. Johnson, a brother-in-law, said of him, "Nothing was too big for him to undertake. Mentally he was a big man and a very creditable man." [249]

"Nothing was too big for him to undertake." It might well have been his epitaph. He had ruled over a vast kingdom, ever developing and expanding it with an eye to improvement. Agriculture had profited; thousands of acres of barley, oats, corn, and garden plants had been cultivated by his station agents. Animal husbandry had been encouraged by his interest in the purchase and raising of superior livestock. The mining industry had benefited through the efficient service of his transportation lines. To the isolated communities of the west his stagecoaches had brought letters, books, magazines, and congressional documents to strengthen the bonds of union with the east, at a time when disruption of communication might have resulted in disruption of the union. And he had patriotically maintained his lines of communication, carrying on under severe financial losses and against almost overwhelming obstacles, as befitted a true stagecoach king.

[249] Atchison (Kans.) *daily free press,* may 17, 1865; Root and Connelley, *Overland stage,* 453; Rusling, *Across America,* 40.

Appendices

Purchases of Holladay at Camp Floyd, Utah
Territory for the third quarter of 1859 [250]

Voucher	Date	Property	Cost
No. 18	July 14	5 horses	$ 160.00
		1 mule	75.00
No. 19	July 15	15 mules	1,237.50
No. 20	July 16	3 mules	240.00
No. 21	July 18	24 mules	2,120.00
No. 22	July 19	40 mules	2,905.00
No. 23	July 20	38 mules	3,630.00
No. 24	July 21	106 mules	8,110.00
No. 25	July 22	60 mules	4,240.00
No. 26	July 23	55 mules	4,040.00
No. 27	July 25	46 mules	4,200.00
No. 28	July 26	46 mules	3,920.00
No. 30	July 27	81 mules	6,820.00
No. 31	July 28	92 mules	8,137.50
No. 32	July 29	171 mules	14,947.50
		2 horses	135.00
No. 33	August	3 mules, 4 wagons 4 double-trees, 8 single-trees 4 sets wheel harness 8 sets lead harness 2 lines lead	400.00
No. 44 (no date)		1 mule	75.00
Total:		782 mules, 7 horses 4 wagons, 12 sets harness 2 lines lead, 4 double-trees 8 single-trees	$65,392.50

[250] Reports of quartermaster-general, 3rd quarter, 1859, abstract L, I, MS. (War department, general accounting department, Washington, D.C.). Holladay gave a draft for $73,267.50 to the army officer for the purchases, but vouchers for only $65,392.00 were found in Washington. In association with two others, Holladay made another purchase on july 29 (voucher 32), of 17 wagons for $510.00. The names of these associates were not legible, but probably were Waller (or Wallis) and Bole (or Ball, or Bale).

Trustees Sale [251]

Whereas, on the twenty-second of november, A.D. 1861, the Central Overland California and Pike's Peak Express company, made, executed, and delivered to the undersigned as trustees, a deed conveying to said trustees all the horses, mules, cattle, coaches, wagons, buggies, sets of harness, hay, grain, provision, lumber, tools, materials, and furniture held and used by said company in carrying the overland mail from Atchison in Kansas, to Salt Lake City in Utah, and from Overland City to Denver, and from Denver to Central City and to Tarryhall, in Colorado territory, together with all the stations on said several roads, which deed is made to secure the payment of a penal bond to Benjamin Holladay, of even date of said deed, for the sum of four hundred thousand dollars and for the performance of conditions of said bond and the covenants of said deed. And whereas, the conditions of said bond and the covenants of said deed have been broken, and said penalty is unpaid; in pursuance of said deed the undersigned as such trustees will on friday, the seventh of march, A.D. 1862, at the Massosoit House in the city of Atchison in the state of Kansas, proceed to sell all the above conveyed property in one body to the highest bidder for cash in hand to satisfy the conditions of said deed.

T. F. Warner)
Rob. L. Pease) *Trustees*

Atchison, February 15, 1862.

---

[251] *Freedom's champion* (Atchison, Kans.), february 15, march 7, 21, 22, 1862.

HOLLADAY STAGE LINE EXPRESS RATES
for freight and treasure in 1865 [252]

FROM NEW YORK TO DENVER

Express freight, for each 100 pounds	$60.75 in currency
Currency, for each $1000	18.75 in currency
Gold, for each $1000	19.75 in currency

FROM ATCHISON TO DENVER

Express freight, for each 100 pounds	$50.00 in currency
Currency, for each $1000	15.00 in currency
Gold, for each $1000	15.00 in currency

---

[252] Atchison (Kans.) *daily free press,* september 7, 1865. The rates from Atchison to Denver were listed as 50c a pound for express freight, one and one-half per cent the currency value for treasure and gold.

EXPRESS ACCOUNTS OF
THE CENTRAL OVERLAND CALIFORNIA
From Fort Kearny, Neb.
Wm. Hudnut, messenger.

No.	Wt.	Value	From whom received			To whom addressed
1]	1 pkg.	$1,802.00	U.S. Express Company			Messrs. Campbell & Jones
2]	1 "	19.50	"	"	"	Dr. J. F. Wisely
3]	1 "		"	"	"	John N. King
4]	1 "	60.00	"	"	"	Charles Britty
5]	1 val. papers		"	"	"	Kountz & Bro.
6]	1 pkg.	250.00	Mr. Clark			Dudley and White

OVERLAND STAGE LINE,
carrying the great through mails
from Atchison to Denver.
Hudnett, messenger.[254]

No.		From whom received	To whom addressed	Destination
7]	1 pa.....	$10,000	U.S. Exp. Co.	C. E. Blakesby	Cent. City
8]	1 pa.....	2,800	—— Do ——	J. H. Malone	—— Do ——
9]	1 pd. coll.	6	—— Do ——	A. Arbor	Denver
10]	1 pa.....	960	—— Do ——	W. Hussey & Co.	—— Do ——
11]	1 pa.....	1,000	—— Do ——	J. G. Mahoney	Cent. City
12]	1 pa.....	50	—— Do ——	J. W. Buchanan	—— Do ——
13]	1 pa.....	50	—— Do ——	R. Teats	—— Do ——
14]	1 pa.....	10,000	—— Do ——	C.A.Cooke&Co.	Denver
15]	1 pa.....	45	—— Do ——	O. C. Bruner	Seneca
16]	1 pd. coll.	250	—— Do ——	J. W. Hugas	Kearney
17]	1 pa.....	50	—— Do ——	Solomon & Bro.	Denver
18]	1 pa.....	700	—— Do ——	J. N. Field	Ft. Kearny
19]	1 pa.....	4,500	—— W.A.G. ——	E. F. Bruce, agt.	—— Do ——
20]	1 pa.....	4,000	—— Do ——	Holladay & Carlyle	—— Do ——

[254] This name was variously spelled, not only Hudnut and Hudnett, but also Hudnet.

A HOLLADAY MESSENGER, 1865 [253]
AND PIKE'S PEAK EXPRESS COMPANY
to Denver, Jan. 5th, 1865
No. 42—Treasure.

Destination	Adv. Chgs.	Our charges local	Collect	Local	Prepaid from Denver	Remarks
1] Denver	$7.50	$27.00	$34.50	....	....	
2] Julesburg		2.00	2.00	....	....	J.F.Wisely
3] Cottonwood	4.00	2.00	6.00	....	....	North
4] Central City	1.00	2.00	3.00	....	....	
5] Denver	4.00	8.00	12.00	....	....	Received 2 warrants K. Bros.
6] Denver		3.75	3.75	....	....	per. F.
	16.50	44.75	61.25			

BEN HOLLADAY, PROPRIETOR
between the Atlantic and Pacific States
Tuesday, Jan'y 3rd, 1865
No. 1. Duplicate.

	Expense	Our charges	Collect	Prepaid charges	Lost
7]	$32.50	$150.00	$182.50		Do
8]		49.00		$49.00	Do
9]		.75		.75	Five Land Warrants
10]	3.25	14.40	17.65		Saved; one lost
11]	3.25	15.00	18.25		Lost
12]		2.00	2.00		Rec'd. Dahler
13]		2.00	2.00		Do. Do.
14]	30.00	150.00	180.00		Do. Do.
15]		1.00	1.00		J. E. Smith
16]		D.H.			Line Bus.
17]		2.00	2.00		Lost
18]		5.00	5.90		Lloyd
19]		D.H.			Line Bus
20]		Do.			Do.

253 U.S. Senate. *Miscellaneous documents*, 46 cong., 2 sess., I, no. 19, 84.

HOLLADAY ORDERS FOR ABBOT-DOWNING STAGE-
COACHES FROM CONCORD, N.H.[255]

(ORDER FOR COACHES APRIL 2, 1864: [orders no.] 768 to 787)

Ben Holladay New York April 2, 1864

Twenty-Nine Passenger inside Stage Coaches SOUTHERN STYLE
not to weigh over 2000 lbs. all complete.

[MS. *memoranda on margin: 4 chg'd July 29/64; 6 dlv'd Aug.
26/64; 6 chg'd Sept. 29/64; 4 chg'd Oct. 22, 1864*]

Bag foot boards & Back Boots with leather sides & flaps

Top seat back of Driver no hind seat

Side lights & Corner Panels – Bunten & prongs both ends

Braces stitched 3¼ wide – Sand boxes cut out at bottom

Axle 2⅛ Tire 1¾x¾ Track 5 ft. 2 C to C

Wheel usual height – Brakes & Springs

Axle top of Perches – Evener Chains & Pole clip straps

Large Candle Lamps wire pattern Middle seat 3 fold

Jacks Stout – Projection Sides & Corner pillars, ironed and bolted.

Ends of bodies Stripped with Iron x to Jacks on Coach 1⅞ or 2 in.
wide.

Paint Bodies Red – Carriages Straw

Letter Overland Stage Line U. S. M.

Russet Leather Lined Leather Curtains

Damask Lined Damask head & fringe

No Driver apron No Top Canvas of any Kind

Six of the above Coaches to be furnished for the Overland Mail
Co. San Francisco, California.

Done in July 1864 Sure no fail

No. 785-787-779-784x-786-781-783+780—782x797

FOR OVERLAND MAIL CO.

Ben Holladay New York Oct. 10-1865

Ten-Nine Passenger inside Stage Coaches

Curtain Quarter End Panel & Side Light

---

255 Burgum, letter to author, 1, 2, 3, MS.

Top Seats Bunten Projection Sides. Prongs both
ends on Sill iron Bag foot board Back Boot Lea
and flaps Perches under axle & stout   sides
Axle 2⅛ tire 1¾x¾ Braces 3¼ wide stitched
Track 5 ft 2 C to C
Wheels usual height, Brakes as usual
Evener chains & Pole Clip Straps. Sand Boxes cut out
Bodies to these to be made to have more room
between back and middle seats. 3 fold seats
End of bodies Strapped with iron x corner Pillars
ironed & bolted at sills Strong. Jacks Stout 1⅞ or
2 in.
Whiffletrees & Lead bars with rings. Pole hook stout wide
Candle Lamps wire Tubes.
   Steps on Brake & None on Body
Paint Bodies Red Carriage Straw
Letter [Overland Stage Line u. s. m.] *run out*
       THE Holladay O.M. & Ex. Co.
Russet Lea Lined Lea Curtain Loose
Damask head & fringe. No apron front
No Canvasses of any kind
                Done February 1-1866

HOLLADAY O. M. & Ex. Co. New York April 20, 1866
[MS. *memorandum on margin: Raynoldi 135, 136, Chg'd July
27, 1866*]
Two-Nine inside Pass. Coach Bodies
Bunten Rolls Sills Projection No Top Railing
Prongs on both Ends E. P. Side Light
Top Seat Bag foot board on one & none on
other but all the iron & c
No racks on either
No Top Railing Wanted to Either
Braces to Both 3¼ wide & Stout
No lamps These coach Bodies were all com-
plete but Front Boot for Driver & Lamps

Paint Bodies Red
Ornament with stripes & c Line as Last
Ten Coaches
Russet Lea Lined Damask heads & Lea
Curtain Damask Lined & fringe
  Straps on top inside No apron
    No Canvasses
          Done at once

STATIONS OF THE ATCHISON–SALT LAKE CITY STAGE LINE [256]

ATCHISON TO FORT KEARNY DIVISION

Miles between stations	Station	Miles from Atchison
10	Lancaster	10
14	Kennekuk	24
12	Kickapoo	36
13	Log Chain	49
11	Seneca	60
12	Laramie Creek	72
12	Guittard's	84
10	Oketo	94
11	Otoe	105
11	Pawnee (Nebraska terr.)	116
14	Grayson's	130
10	Big Sandy	140
14	Thompson's	154
14	Kiowa	168
12	Little Blue	180
13	Liberty Farm	193
15	Lone Tree	208
10	Thirty-two-mile Creek	218
12	Summit	230
13	Hook's	243
10	Fort Kearny	253

[256] U.S. House. *Executive documents,* 38 cong., 2 sess., VIII, no. 24, 10; Root and Connelley, *Overland stage,* 93, 101, 102, 167; Hafen, *Overland mail,* 343, for Julesburg to Granger division; Atchison (Kans.) *daily free press,* september 2, 1865, for post-offices between Atchison and Denver; Omaha *Nebraskian,* may 18, 1866, for stations from Omaha, 1866. Route 14258, as advertised in 1863, had Fort Halleck as a station between Elk Mountain and Medicine Bow, and South Bend for Ham's Fork.

FORT KEARNY TO DENVER DIVISION

Miles between stations	Station	Miles from Atchison
0	Fort Kearny	253
10	Platte	263
11	Craig	274
15	Plum Creek	289
15	Willow Island	304
14	Midway	318
15	Gilman's	333
17	Cottonwood Springs	350
15	Cold Springs	365
14	Fremont Springs	379
11	Elkhorn	390
14	Alkali Lake	404
12	Sand Hill	416
11	Diamond Springs	427
15	South Platte	442
14	Julesburg (Colorado terr.)	456
12	Antelope	468
13	Spring Hill	481
13	Dennison's	494
12	Valley	506
15	Kelley's	521
12	Beaver Creek	533
20	Bijou	553
16	Fremont's Orchard	569
16	Eagle's Nest	580
12	Latham	592
15	Big Bend	607
17	Fort Lupton	624
15	Pierson's	639
14	Denver	653

Denver to Salt Lake City division

Miles between stations	Station	Miles from Atchison
0	Denver	653
11	Child's	664
12	Boone's	676
18	Little Thompson	694
8	Big Thompson	702
16	Laporte	718
10	Bouer	728
12	Cherokee	740
12	Virginia Dale	752
15	Willow Springs (Dakota terr.)	767
15	Big Laramie	782
14	Little Laramie	796
17	Cooper Creek	813
11	Rock Creek	824
17	Medicine Bow	841
8	Elk Mountain	849
14	Pass Creek	863
16	North Platte	889
14	Sage Creek	903
10	Pine Grove	913
9	Bridger's Pass	922
10	Sulphur Springs	932
11	Waskie	943
13	Duck Lake	956
12	Dug Springs	968
15	Laclede	983
12	Big Pond	995
14	Black Buttes	1009
14	Rock Point	1023
14	Salt Wells	1037
14	Rock Springs	1051
15	Green River	1066
14	Lone Tree	1080
18	Ham's Fork	1098

Miles between stations	Station	Miles from Atchison
12	Church Buttes	1110
8	Millerville	1118
13	Fort Bridger	1131
12	Muddy	1143
10	Quaking Asp Springs	1153
10	Bear River	1163
10	Needle Rock (Utah terr.)	1173
10	Echo Canyon	1183
10	Hanging Rock	1193
10	Weaver	1203
12	Daniel's	1215
11	Kimball's	1226
15	Mountain Dale	1241
14	Salt Lake City	1255

STATIONS BETWEEN JULESBURG AND GRANGER
(used early in 1862)

Julesburg
Mud Springs
Fort Mitchell
Fort Laramie (Idaho terr.)
Horseshoe

Platte Bridge (Fort Casper)
Three Crossings
Big Sandy
Granger

POST-OFFICES BETWEEN ATCHISON AND DENVER

Atchison
Lancaster
Huron
Kennekuk
Grenada
Log Chain
Seneca
Ash Point
Guittard's
Marysville (about 100 miles from Atchison)

Big Sandy (150 miles from Atchison)
Valley City (junction of Nebraska City and Atchison roads)
Fort Kearny (253 miles from Atchison)
Kearney City (255 miles)
Plum Creek (288 miles)
Cottonwood Springs (350 miles)
Julesburg (456 miles, assorting office for Fort Laramie, Platte Bridge, and Sweet-water)
Junction House (550 miles from Atchison)
Living Springs (45 miles from Denver)

Distances of the Stations from Omaha, 1866

Omaha to Fort Kearny Division

Omaha to Elkhorn	23 miles
Omaha to Fremont	38 miles
Omaha to North Bend	53 miles
Omaha to Buchanan	64 miles
Omaha to Skinner's	75 miles
Omaha to Columbus	86 miles
Omaha to Eagle Island	106 miles
Omaha to Junction Ranch	114 miles
Omaha to Lone Tree	132 miles
Omaha to Grand Island	154 miles
Omaha to Lamb's	162 miles
Omaha to Wood River farm	177 miles
Omaha to Fort Kearny	193 miles

Omaha to Distant Points on Holladay Lines

Omaha to Julesburg	302 miles
Omaha to Bridger's Pass	757 miles
Omaha to Fort Bridger	900 miles
Omaha to Great Salt Lake City	1060 miles
Omaha to Bannock City	1466 miles
Omaha to Virginia City	1549 miles
Omaha to Boise City	1860 miles

Stations on the Smoky Hill Division in 1866

Miles between stations	Station	Miles from Junction City
12	Chapman's Creek	12
13	Aberlene City [Abilene]	25
10	Solomon*	35
10	Owens	45
13	Spring Creek	58
14	Rocky Ranch	72
10	Ellsworth	82
10	Buffalo Creek	92

Miles between stations	Station	Miles from Junction City
9	Wilson's Creek*	101
8	Bunker Hill	109
8	Fossil Creek	117
10	Walker's Creek	127
12	Big Creek*	139
9	Look Out	148
12	Stormy Hollow	160
11	White Rock	171
10	Downer*	181
11	Castle Rock	192
8	Grinnel Springs	200
13	Chalk Bluffs	213
8	Carlyle Hall	221
10	Monument*	231
12	Smoky Hill	243
10	Russell Springs	253
14	Henshaw Springs	267
11	Pond Creek*	278
11	Goose Creek	289
10	Big Timber	299
15	Cheyenne Wells*	314
13	Deering's Wells	327
13	Big Springs*	340
10	David's Wells	350
10	Hugo Springs	360
13	Willow Springs	373
11	Lake Station*	384
9	Cedar Point	393
8	Fairmount	401
9	Benham Springs	410
11	Bijou Springs*	421
10	Kiowa	431
12	Box Elder	443
12	Toll Gate	455
10	Denver	465

* Home or eating stations.

LOSSES OF HOLLADAY IN 1862 AND 1863
according to testimony before the Committee on Claims, 1880 [257]

Station	Date	Losses	Value
Green River	April 1862	100 sacks barley	$1500.00
		(10,000 lbs. at 15c)	
		50 sacks oats	750.00
		(5000 lbs. at 15c)	
		5 horses at $200	1000.00
		6 sets harness at $20	120.00
		120 sacks oats at $5	600.00
		480 empty sacks at 60c	288.00
		Damage to station	600.00
Sweetwater Bridge	April 18	8 mules and horses at $200	
			1600.00
Horse Creek	May 13	5 horses at $175	875.00
		18 mules at $225	4050.00
Red Buttes [258]	April 1	15 mules and horses at $175	
			2625.00
	April 21	6 mules and horses at $175	
			1050.00
Platte Bridge	March	13 mules at $150	1950.00
Big Sandy	April	18 mules at $225	4050.00
		4 horses at $225	900.00
		1 four-horse set of harness	110.00
	June 7	4 mules at $200	800.00
		20 sacks oats at $5	100.00
		3 tons hay at $30	90.00
		Damage to station	500.00
Dry Sandy	March 15	2 mules at $200	400.00
	June	Damage to station	500.00

[257] U.S. Senate. *Report,* 46 cong., 2 sess., I, no. 216, 10-22; *Miscellaneous documents,* 46 cong., 2 sess., I, no. 19, 1-88.

[258] J. A. Slade, division agent from Julesburg to Sweetwater, reported the loss at Horse Creek to have been on march 23, 1862, and the second loss at Red Buttes on april 24.

Station	Date	Losses	Value
Muddy	June 12	4 mules at $200	800.00
Bear River	June	2 horses at $100	200.00
Little Sandy	June	30 sacks oats at $5	150.00
		Damage to station	500.00
Pacific Springs	June	Damage to station	500.00
Wells	April 20	2 horses at $150	300.00
Rocky Ridge	April 18	6 mules at $200	1200.00
Split Rock	March 1	10 mules at $200	2000.00
		1 horse at $200	200.00
		12 sets single harness at $20	240.00
	March 30	7 mules at $200	1400.00
		8 sets single harness at $20	160.00
	May	Damage to station	500.00
Three Crossings	April 16	22 mules and horses at $225	4950.00
		10 sets stage harness at $110	1100.00
		3 head oxen at $50	150.00
Near			
Three Crossings	April 17	9 mules at $200	1800.00
		9 sets harness at $110	990.00
		Damage to 2 coaches	500.00
Three Crossings	May	Damage to station	500.00
Plant's	April 18	5 mules at $200	1000.00
		4 horses at $225	900.00
	April 20	20 sets four-horse harness at $110	2200.00
		2 mules at $200	400.00
Ice Springs	April 23	10 mules at $200	2000.00
		1 cow, 1 ox, at $50	100.00
		5 sets four-horse harness at $110	550.00
	May	Damage to station	500.00
Strawberry	May 23	35 sacks barley (3500 lbs. at 15c)	525.00

Station	Date	Losses	Value
Upper crossings of Sweetwater	May	18 sacks barley (1800 lbs. at 15c)	270.00
Sweetwater	May	Damage to station	500.00
Taken off line	April 20	10 mules	(no estimate)
Near Fort Halleck	1863	173 horses and 34 mules	41,400.00

TOTAL 399 horses and mules, 220 sacks oats, 153 sacks barley, 3 tons hay, 71 sets harness, 4 oxen, 9 stations and 2 stagecoaches damaged $92,943.00

LOSSES OF HOLLADAY FROM JULY 1864 TO FEBRUARY 1865 according to testimony before the Committee on Claims, 1880

Station	Losses	Value
Alkali	250 sacks corn (28,000 lbs. at 20c)	$5600.00
	20 tons hay at $40	800.00
American Ranch	58 oxen at $100	5800.00
	Barn destroyed	1500.00
	30 tons hay at $50	1500.00
	227 sacks corn (25,424 lbs. at 22c)	5593.28
	2 horses at $250	500.00
	2 sets four-horse harness at $110	220.00
	8 stage horses at $250	2000.00
Antelope	House, barn, and corral burned	5000.00
	25 tons hay at $50	1250.00
	125 sacks corn (14,000 lbs. at 20c)	2800.00
Beaver Creek	75 sacks corn (8400 lbs. at 22c)	1848.00
	1 stage horse	250.00
Bijou	48 sacks corn (5376 lbs. at 22c)	1182.72
	7 tons hay at $50	350.00
Box Elder	10 tons hay at $50	500.00
Cold Spring	40 sacks corn (4480 lbs. at 20c)	896.00
	15 tons hay at $40	600.00
Craig	250 sacks corn (28,000 lbs. at 20c)	5600.00
	29 oxen at $100	2900.00
Dennison	Barn and corral burned	2500.00
	25 tons hay at $50	1250.00
	200 sacks corn (22,400 lbs. at 22c)	4928.00

Station	Losses	Value
Diamond Springs	250 sacks corn (28,000 lbs. at 20c)	5600.00
	15 tons hay at $40	600.00
Elkhorn	65 sacks corn (7280 lbs. at 20c)	1456.00
	10 tons hay at $40	400.00
	Station burned	3500.00
Gilman's	30 sacks corn (3360 lbs. at 20c)	672.00
Julesburg [259]	1 mule	100.00
	1 set four-horse harness	120.00
	2 bales clothing	1500.00
	Barns, sheds, warehouses, telegraph office, blacksmith shop, houses burned	35000.00
	Damage to coach	500.00
	30 tons hay at $50	1500.00
	3500 sacks corn (392,000 lbs. at 20c)	78400.00
	Provisions and stores	2000.00
	1 horse	200.00
Junction	100 sacks corn (11,200 lbs. at 22c)	2464.00
	5 stage horses at $250	1250.00
Junction Ranch	10 tons hay at $50	500.00
Kiowa	15 tons hay at $50	750.00
Liberty Farm	Stagecoach burned	1200.00
Liberty Town	2 sets double harness at $110	220.00
Little Blue	Furniture and grain destroyed	2000.00
	2 horses killed on road at $200	400.00
Living Springs	5 tons hay at $50	250.00
Lone Tree	9 horses at $200	1800.00
	5 horses killed in escaping from Indians	1000.00
	Station burned	1000.00
Lupton	1 stage horse	250.00
Midway	30 sacks corn (3360 lbs. at 20c)	672.00
	15 tons hay at $40	600.00
	Dishes and furniture destroyed	500.00

[259] Captain Murphy and G. H. Carlyle valued the mule at $200. Lieutenant J. S. Brewer, Company F, Second Iowa cavalry, reported that he saw many horses with a B.H. brand after the troops took them from an Arapaho band in august 1865.

Station	Losses	Value
Muddy	1500 lbs. corn at 12c	180.00
Murray	100 sacks corn (11,200 lbs. at 22c)	2464.00
Pawnee Ranch	4 horses at $200	800.00
Platte	4 horses at $350	1400.00
	250 sacks corn (28,000 lbs. at 20c)	5600.00
	10 tons hay at $40	400.00
Plum Creek	15 tons hay at $40	600.00
	250 sacks corn (28,000 lbs. at 20c)	5600.00
Rock Bluff	7 tons hay at $50	350.00
Sand Hill	250 sacks corn (28,000 lbs. at 20c)	5600.00
	15 tons hay at $40	600.00
	Station burned [260]	2500.00
Spring Hill	House, barns, furniture destroyed	6000.00
	20 tons hay at $50	1000.00
	90 sacks corn (10,080 lbs. at 22c)	2217.60
Summit	Station, furniture, and bedding destroyed	2500.00
	200 bushels corn (11,200 lbs. at 12c)	1344.00
Thirty-two-mile Creek	Furniture, crockery, stores destroyed	2500.00
Toll Gate	20 tons hay at $50	1000.00
Valley	20 tons hay at $50	1000.00
Willow Island	50 sacks corn (5600 lbs. at 20c)	1120.00
	10 tons hay at $40	400.00
Lost on road	2 stage horses and harness	450.00
TOTAL		$247,397.60

HOLLADAY PROPERTY TAKEN BY U.S. SOLDIERS
from October 1864 to December 1865
according to testimony of Otis, Street, Carlyle, and Reynolds, Holladay employees

Station	Losses	Value
Fort Kearny	29 oxen at $100	$2900.00
Julesburg	100 cords wood at $50	5000.00

[260] Only two employees listed this loss, and it probably was not included in the total losses as figured by the congressional committee.

Station	Losses	Value
On the route	Grain, hay, wood, houses and stables used for fuel	22,100.00

TOTAL		$30,000.00

LOSSES OF HOLLADAY DURING SPRING AND SUMMER OF 1865
according to testimony before the Committee on Claims, 1880

Station	Date	Losses	Value
Bridger's Pass	May 19	Flour and Sharp's rifle	100.00
	May 26	9 horses at $200	1800.00
		8 sets single harness at $30	240.00
		Supplies	100.00
Cooper's Creek	July 1865	1 pony	50.00
		Corral, windows, doors, cooking and box stove destroyed	390.00
Elk Mountain	June 1865	22 mules at $200	4400.00
		4 horses at $225	900.00
		2 ponies at $50	100.00
Little Laramie	August 1865	Station and corral destroyed	3500.00
Medicine Bow	July 1865	2 ponies at $50	100.00
		Corral destroyed	150.00
Murray's	August 1865	15 tons hay at $50	750.00
Pine Grove	June 9	2 sets harness and coal stove damaged	200.00
Rock Creek	July 1865	1 pony	50.00
		Corral destroyed	250.00
Sage Creek	May 22	9 horses at $200	1800.00
	June 8	5 horses at $200	1000.00
	September 4	1 set four-horse harness cut to pieces	120.00
		Station and barn burned	2500.00
		2 men killed	
Stonewall	August 1865	2 yoke oxen at $100	200.00

Bibliography

AMERICAN almanac and repository of useful knowledge (Boston, 1830-61), 32 vols.

ANGEL, Myron. History of the state of Nevada (Oakland, 1881).

ARMY and navy journal (New York), II, III.

ATCHISON daily free press, 1865, 1866.

ATCHISON daily globe, 1894.

[ATCHISON] freedom's champion, 1861, 1862.

ATCHISON union, 1859, 1860, 1861.

BAKER, Julian, former stagecoach repairer for Ben Holladay. Letter to author, MS. (August 21, 1935; files of author).

BANCROFT, Henry Howe. History of Nevada, Colorado, and Wyoming, 1540-1888 (San Francisco, 1890).

———— History of Utah (San Francisco, 1889).

BANNING, William, and George Hugh Banning. Six horses (New York, 1928).

BARBER, John W., and Henry Howe. All the western states and territories (Cincinnati, 1867).

BARNES, Demas. From the Atlantic to the Pacific overland (New York, 1866).

BIRGE, Julius C. The awakening of the desert (Boston, 1912).

BLACK HAWK [Colorado territory] mining journal, 1863, 1864, 1865, 1866.

BOGART, Ernest Ludlow. The economic history of the United States (New York, 1907).

[BOISE] Idaho daily statesman, 1923.

BOWLES, Samuel. Across the continent (New York, 1866).

———— Our new west (Hartford, 1870).

BRADLEY, Glenn D. Story of the pony express (Chicago, 1913).

BROSNAN, C. J. History of the state of Idaho (Chicago, 1926).

BROWN, Jennie Broughton. Fort Hall on the Oregon trail (Caldwell, 1932).

BURGUM, Edwin G., son of former stagecoach painter for Ben Holladay. Letter to author, MS. (July 20, 1936; files of author).

BURTON, Richard F. The city of the saints and across the Rocky mountains to California (New York, 1862).

[CAMP DOUGLAS, Utah territory] daily union vedette, 1865, 1866.

[CENTRAL CITY, Colorado territory] tri-weekly miner's register, 1862; daily miner's register, 1866.

CLAMPITT, John W. Echoes from the Rocky mountains (Chicago, 1889).

CLEMENS, Samuel (Mark Twain). Roughing it (Hartford, 1872).

COLORADO territory legislative laws (Central City, 1866).

COMAN, Katherine. Economic beginnings of the far west (New York, 1925).

CONNELLEY, William Elsey. Doniphan's expedition (Topeka, 1907).

CONTRACT book, 1847-1851, 1855-1856, MS. (Archives of Fort Meyer, Virginia, quartermaster-general's department).

COUTANT, C. G. The history of Wyoming (Laramie, 1899), 3 vols.

DAWSON scrap-book (Newspaper and magazine clippings, library of state historical and natural history society of Colorado, Denver), IV, V, XIV.

[DENVER] daily commonwealth and republican, 1863.

[DENVER] weekly commonwealth and republican, 1863.

[DENVER] Rocky mountain news, 1860, 1862, 1863, 1864, 1865, 1866.

DENVER times, 1915.

DIXON, William Hepworth. New America (London, 1867), 2 vols.

ELLIOTT, Wallace W. History of Idaho territory (San Francisco, 1884).

ELWELL, R. F. "The story of the overland mail," in Frontier days, edited by Oliver G. Swan (Philadelphia, 1928).

GHENT, W.J. The road to Oregon (New York, 1929).

GOLD HILL [Nevada territory] daily news, 1865.

GRINNELL, George Bird. The fighting Cheyennes (New York, 1915).

HAFEN, LeRoy R. The overland mail, 1849-1869 (Cleveland, the Arthur H. Clark company, 1926).

HARLOW, Alvin F. Old waybills: the romance of the express companies (New York, 1934).

HARPER's new monthly magazine (New York), xxxv.

HEBARD, Grace R. The pathbreakers from river to ocean (Glendale, the Arthur H. Clark company, 1933).

HOLLADAY, Ben, heirs of, vs. the United States et al. Motion of the claimants to set aside order of dismissal, MS. (Court of claims, Ind. deps. no. 218, Washington, D.C).

HOLLADAY, Hattie, wife of William, nephew of Ben Holladay. Interview with author, MS. (Weston, 1935; files of author).

HOUCK, Louis. A history of Idaho (Chicago, 1920).

—— A history of Missouri (Chicago, 1908).

HUGHES, Bela M. Letter to John Doniphan, MS. (May 2, 1892; library of state historical and natural history society of Colorado).

HULBERT, Archer B. The paths of inland commerce (Chronicles of America series, New Haven, 1921).

INMAN, Colonel Henry. The old Santa Fé trail (Topeka, 1916).

JUNCTION CITY [Kansas] union, 1865, 1866.

KANSAS CITY [Missouri] times, 1911, 1935.

KANSAS scrap-book (Newspaper and magazine clippings, library of Kansas state historical society, Topeka), II, VIII, XII.

KANSAS state historical society collections (Topeka, 1886, 1904), III, VIII.

KANSAS territorial laws (Lawrence, 1860).

[LAWRENCE] daily Kansas state journal, 1865.

LEAVENWORTH daily conservative, 1861, 1862, 1863, 1864, 1866.

LEAVENWORTH times, 1863.

[LEAVENWORTH] weekly Leavenworth herald, 1859, 1860.

LETTER book, no. 45, 1852-1853, MS. (Archives of Fort Meyer, Virginia, quartermaster-general's department).

LIBERTY [Missouri] tribune, 1851.

McCLURE's magazine (New York), XXVI, no. 1.

MAJORS, Alexander. Seventy years on the frontier (Chicago, 1893).

[MANHATTAN] Kansas radical, 1866.

[MARYSVILLE, Kansas] Marshall county news, 1931.

MARYSVILLE [Kansas] enterprise, 1866.

MEXICAN war claims, MS. (Archives of Fort Meyer, Virginia, quartermaster-general's department).

MISSOURI historical review (Columbia), XV, XVII, XXI, XXV.

MORTON, J. Sterling. Illustrated history of Nebraska (Lincoln, 1905-6), 2 vols.

MUNSON, Lynn E. "Pioneer life on American frontier," in Journal of American history (New Haven), I.

NEBRASKA CITY news, 1862, 1865, 1866.

NEBRASKA state historical society collections (Lincoln, 1911, 1919), XVI, XIX.

OMAHA daily herald, 1865, 1866.

OMAHA Nebraskian, 1864, 1865.

OMAHA weekly herald, 1865, 1866.

OMAHA weekly republican, 1864, 1865, 1866.

PARSONS, Eugene. The making of Colorado (Chicago, 1908).

PAXSON, Frederick Logan. The last American frontier (New York, 1910).

PAXTON, William. Annals of Platte county, Missouri (Kansas City, 1897).

PHILATELIC gossip (Holton, Kansas), VIII.

POLLINGER, E. M., stagecoach driver for Ben Holladay. Letter to Colonel Callaway, MS. (Helena, may 28, 1904; files of Montana state historical society).

POSS, Maude Barton, grandniece of Ben Holladay. Interview with author, MS. (Weston, 1935; files of author).

QUARTERMASTER-GENERAL's book, 1865, 1867, MS. (Archives of Fort Meyer, Virginia, quartermaster-general's department).

QUARTERMASTER-GENERAL's reports, 1820-1856, third quarter of 1859, MS. (War department, general accounting department, Washington, D.C.).

RADER, Perry S. The civil government of the United States and
the state of Missouri (Columbia, 1898).

REGISTER of beef contracts, 1820-1856, MS. (Archives of Fort
Meyer, Virginia, quartermaster-general's department).

RICHARDSON, Albert D. Beyond the Mississippi (Hartford, 1867).

RIEGEL, Robert E. America moves west (New York, 1930).

ROOT, Frank A., and William E. Connelley. The overland stage to
California (Topeka, 1901).

RUSLING, James F. Across America (New York, 1874).

——— The great west and the Pacific coast (New York, 1877).

SACRAMENTO daily union, 1858, 1862, 1863, 1864, 1865.

[ST. JOSEPH, Missouri] catholic tribune, 1895.

[ST. LOUIS] Missouri republican, 1858.

[ST. LOUIS] weekly Missouri democrat, 1858.

[SAN FRANCISCO] alta California, 1853.

SAN FRANCISCO daily evening bulletin, 1860, 1861, 1862, 1863,
1864, 1865, 1866.

SAUNDERS, Arthur C. The history of Bannock county, Idaho
(Pocatello, 1915).

SMILEY, Jerome C. History of Denver (Denver, 1903).

STONE, Wilbur Fisk. History of Colorado (Chicago, 1918), 4 vols.

[THE DALLES, Oregon] weekly mountaineer, 1864, 1865, 1866.

TOPEKA tribune, 1866.

TOPONCE, Alexander. Reminiscences (Salt Lake City, 1923).

TRAILS clippings (Newspaper and magazine clippings, library of
Kansas state historical society, Topeka), I, II.

TULLIDGE, E. W. History of Salt Lake City (Salt Lake City,
1892), 3 vols.

TWOMBLY, George, former stagecoach driver for Ben Holladay.
Interview with author, MS. (Denver, 1934; files of author).

[VIRGINIA CITY, Montana territory] Montana democrat, 1866.

U.S. CONGRESSIONAL globe, 34 cong., 3 sess., appendix.

——— 36 cong., 2 sess., part I.

U.S. DEPARTMENT of interior, office of Indian affairs, commissioner's annual reports, 1865, 1866 for Utah and Montana territories; 1866 for upper Arkansas agency (files 1862, no. 43).

U.S. House. Executive documents, 33 cong., 2 sess., no. 86 (mail contracts).

—— 35 cong., I sess., XI, no. 96 (abstract of offers for carrying the mails).

—— 35 cong., 2 sess., XI, no. 109 (mail contracts).

—— 40 cong., 2 sess., XV, no. 201 (contracts with Benjamin Holladay, 1864).

U.S. House. Reports, 47 cong., I sess., IV, no. 1182.

U.S. Medical histories of posts, MS. (War department, old records division, Washington, D.C.).

U.S. Military order, St. Louis, headquarters, department of Missouri, august 2, october 23, 1866, MS. (Archives of Fort Meyer, Virginia, quartermaster-general's department).

U.S. Military stations and posts, MS. (Archives of Fort Meyer, Virginia).

U.S. Muster rolls, 1866, MS. (War department, old records division, Washington, D.C.).

U.S. Post history, Camp Lander, Idaho territory, MS. (War department, old records division, Washington, D.C.).

U.S. Post returns, 1862, 1863, 1864, 1865, MS. (War department, old records division, Washington, D.C.).

U.S. Postmaster-general's annual report of:

1857, Sen. Ex. docs., 35 cong., I sess., IV, no. 11.

1858, Sen. Ex. docs., 35 cong., 2 sess., IV, no. 1, part 4.

1860, Sen. Ex. docs., 36 cong., 2 sess., III, part 3, no. 1.

1861, Sen. Ex. docs., 37 cong., 2 sess., III, part 3, no. 1.

1864, House Ex. docs., 38 cong., 2 sess., V, no. 1.

1865, House Ex. docs., 39 cong., I sess., VI, no. 1.

1866, House Ex. docs., 39 cong., 2 sess., IV, no. 1.

U.S. Senate. Miscellaneous documents, 46 cong., 2 sess., I, no. 19.

U.S. Senate. Reports, 44 cong., 2 sess., no. 583.

——, 46 cong., 2 sess., I, no. 216.

U.S. Special reports of:

1865, House Ex. doc., 38 cong., 2 sess., VIII, no. 24.

1868, House Ex. doc., 40 cong., 2 sess., XV, no. 201.

1880, Sen. Ex. doc., 46 cong., 2 sess., V, no. 211.

U.S. STATUTES at large (Boston, 1855-1863), X, XI, XII.

VISSCHER, William Lightfoot. A thrilling and truthful history of the pony express (Chicago, 1908).

WAR of the rebellion: compilation of official records of union and confederate armies (Washington, 1880-1901 [1902]), series I, XLI, part III; XLVIII, part I; L, part II.

WARE, Eugene. Indian war of 1864 (Topeka, 1911).

WALLA WALLA [Washington territory] statesman, 1865.

[WASHINGTON, D.C.] daily national intelligencer, 1864.

WILDER, Daniel W. Annals of Kansas (Topeka, 1875).

WINTHER, Oscar O. Express and stagecoach days in California (Stanford university, 1936).

Index

Index

Daniel's station (Utah territory): 292

David's Wells (Colorado territory): 294

Deer Creek (Dakota territory): 171, 172, 208, 226

Deering's Wells (Colorado territory): 294

Denison, George: 122

Dennison, Postmaster-general William: 129

Dennison's station (Colorado territory): 290, 297

Denver (Colorado): 54, 162, 166, 184; on stage routes, 55, 61, 65, 71, 79, 80, 95, 97, 103, 243-46, 290, 291, 294; stage service, 83, 84, 86, 96, 113, 115, 139, 140, 142; ticket office, 88, 89; game near, 100; stations from, 102, 103; city in *1863*, 108, *frontispiece;* fares, 111, 112, 126, 135, 142, 143; mail service, 123, 124, 193, 195, 255-56; express, 125, 136; Holladay's contracts, 133, 134, 302; Holladay in, 175; Indian hostilities near, 190, 198, 199, 201-207, 208, 210, 213, 214; city in *1868,* 247; railroad, 255

Devil's Gate (Utah territory): 170, 178

Diamond Springs (Nebraska territory): 290, 298

Dinsmore, W.H: 122

Dixson, William: 256

Dodge, General Grenville F: 209

Doniphan, Colonel Alexander: 22, 29, 274

Doty, General: 183

Doty, Superintendent James Duane: 170

Downer (Kansas): 294

Downey, Frances: 265

Downing, Major Jacob: 190

Drake, Lieutenant John: 232

Drew, Major George A: 219

Drivers: 71-76, 82

Dry Sandy (Dakota territory): 169, 295

Duck Lake (Dakota territory): 214, 291

Duck Springs (Dakota territory): 214

Dug Springs (Dakota territory): 291

Dunn, Lieutenant W.K: 190

Dye, George: 24

EAGLE ISLAND (Nebraska territory): 293

Eagle's Nest (Colorado territory): 290

East Bannock (Montana territory): 150

Eaton, Superintendent Isaac: 177

Echo canyon (Utah territory): 93, 101, 292

Edgerton (Missouri): 31

Eldorado (Nebraska territory): 141

Elk Mountain (Dakota territory): 213, 291, 300

Elkhorn (Nebraska territory): 109, 142, 290, 293, 298

Elking, P.D: 139

Ellsworth (Kansas): 293

Emery, Mrs: 110

Empire City (Colorado territory): 133

Employees: on Holladay line, 71-78, 80

Equipment and supplies: 92, 165-67, 177, 199-200, 207, 228

Evans, George: 184

Evans, Governor John: 191, 192

Express: business, 78-79, 124, 125,